D1044175

SEXUALITY

Encounters, Identities, and Relationships

Edited by
Carol Warren

SAGE PUBLICATIONS   *Beverly Hills / London*   **1977**

The material in this publication originally appeared as a special issue of URBAN LIFE (Volume 5, Number 3, October 1976). The Publisher would like to acknowledge the assistance of the journal's editor, John Irwin, and the special issue editor, Carol Warren, in making this edition possible.

For information address:

SAGE PUBLICATIONS, INC.
275 South Beverly Drive
Beverly Hills, California 90212

SAGE PUBLICATIONS LTD
28 Banner Street
London EC1Y 8QE, England

Printed in the United States of America
International Standard Book Number 0-8039-0857-1
Library of Congress Catalog Card Number 77-80074

FIRST PRINTING

CONTENTS

SEXUALITY

Encounters, Identities, and Relationships

CAROL WARREN is Assistant Professor at the University of Southern California. She has written several books and articles in the area of homosexuality and sexuality, including *Identity and Community in the Gay World* (1974) and *Understanding Sexual Interaction* (1977, with Joann S. DeLora). Her current area of interest is mental health and the law.

SEXUALITY:
ENCOUNTERS, IDENTITIES,
AND RELATIONSHIPS
Editor's Introduction

SEXUALITY IN OUR WESTERN SOCIETY is sociologically diverse, encompassing not only behavior but also identities, settings, and relationships. The papers in this volume reflect this sociological diversity, including interview and field observation research on bisexual and lesbian identity, homosexuals' relationships with their families, sexual crime and victimization, prostitution, and sexual encounters in pickup bars.

Sexual encounters in our culture take place in both public and private settings. As Cloyd's article on pickup bars and Rasmussen and Kuhn's on massage parlors indicate, the public or preliminary aspects of sexual encounters are far more available to the observer-researcher than the private phases. Both articles, therefore, provide information on the variety of ways in which sexual encounters are initiated, staged, avoided, or facilitated, rather than on the "payoff" of genital encounter.

These articles also indicate the variety of ways in which sexual encounters are or are not lodged historically in enduring relationships between persons. In massage parlors, sexual encounters may occur once or

AUTHOR'S NOTE: An earlier version of this paper was presented at the first annual meeting of the International Academy of Sex Research, Stony Brook, New York, November 1975.

several times between customer and masseuse, but remain within the limited emotional and physical setting of the parlor. As both Cloyd and Rasmussen and Kuhn note, however, sexuality retains the potential for emotional "spillover" beyond the original setting. Therefore, special techniques are developed for keeping impersonal sexual encounters impersonal. In both articles relationships beyond the research setting appear as a subsidiary theme. The prostitute's work at the massage parlor is often separated from her continuing emotional relationships with boyfriend or husband; sometimes she keeps the details or existence of her work hidden from him. Some of the customers at pickup bars are married to persons in other cities, while the spouses of others are temporarily out of town.

Both Ponse's and Carrier's articles deal with aspects of homosexuals' and lesbians' relationships with their families. Carrier's article—which gives an interesting cross-cultural perspective on early homosexual experience— documents the initiation and continuation of sexual relationships between younger and older male relatives. Both his and Ponse's articles discuss the difficulties experienced by gays in dealing with family relationships either by secrecy or disclosure of their gayness.

Rasmussen and Kuhn's, Ponse's, Blumstein and Schwartz's, and Carrier's articles indicate the many ways in which sexual encounters are linked to personal and social identity. Ponse's article documents the ways in which social stigma and secrecy operate to cement lesbians' identities, both by estranging them from the larger society and by facilitating the development of lesbian communities and reference groups. Rasmussen's article, too, illustrates the impact of the setting—the massage parlor—and of the prostitution stigma on the identities of masseuses.

Blumstein and Schwartz's article is concerned with identity in the context of male bisexuality. Bisexuality poses a different sociological and personal problem in our culture than lesbianism, since it is a less socially legitimate identity than either heterosexuality or gayness. Bisexuals find themselves stigmatized both by the straight society and by the gay community. However, both Ponse's and Blumstein and Schwartz's articles demonstrate that a bisexual identity is interpreted as politically superior and enlightened among some persons who might otherwise adopt a heterosexual or gay identity.

Carrier's article is concerned not only with gay or homosexual identity but also with the relative masculinity or femininity of role style. The lower-class Mexican gays whom Carrier observed and interviewed were raised in a culture in which male and female gender identity was highly distinct, and male and female role style clearly differentiated and reinforced. Male homosexuals, like Mexican heterosexuals, therefore tend to adopt a clear-cut masculine or feminine role style.

In all articles discussed thus far, the sexual encounters and preliminaries—singles bars, apartments, massage parlors, or gay institutions—take place in the context of mutual consent and desire. The Davis article on "flashers," on the other hand, involves the unexpected (and illegal) display of male genitals to unsuspecting females. Because of the unexpected character of "indecent exposure," the meanings and reactions experienced and expressed by the "victims" are much more problematic than the more ritualized meanings and reactions displayed in structured interactions such as the pickup bar. Meanings and processes become more salient in victims' experiences and as a research topic than do identities or relationships.

Despite the variability of these six articles on sexuality, they are unified—either implicitly or explicitly—by the concept of stigma. This is because none is concerned with our society's ideal sexuality: married, emotionally invested, and heterosexually identified relationships. Any type of sexuality deviating from this ideal is stigmatized to a degree ranging from slightly tainted to utterly horrendous. In Cloyd's article, some of the participants experienced guilt, shame, or disgust at the one-night-stand or pickup activities involved, since these activities are somewhat stigmatizing—especially for females. At the somewhat more stigmatized pole of the stigma spectrum are homosexuality, lesbianism, and bisexuality, whether expressed in sexual behavior, identity, or relationships. Indeed, almost all the activities touched upon in this article are illegal in some jurisdictions, including prostitution, indecent exposure, oral or anal sex (homosexual or heterosexual), and premarital or extramarital sexual activity.

Stigma is focused upon directly in the articles on indecent exposure and on homosexuality, bisexuality, and lesbianism. The Davis article, in fact, is an empirical investigation of the degree to which flashers are stigmatized by victims, whose reactions vary from fright and horror to humor and pity. Many flasher victims, like members of straight society, assume that flashing is an indicator of moral essence just as many straights assume that sexual behavior is cemented to identity. Thus, in our society, sexuality is fraught with more than behavioral implications. As this volume demonstrates, sexual behavior reverberates in many corners of participants' lives—beyond interactions and settings into the essential dialectic of self and society.

—*Carol Warren*
University of Southern California

PAUL K. RASMUSSEN is currently an advanced graduate student at the University of California, San Diego. He is in the process of completing his doctoral dissertation on the subject of prostitution. His major areas of interest are deviance, marriage and family, social psychology, and mass communications.

LAUREN L. KUHN is currently a graduate student in the Department of Social Work at San Diego State University. She is completing her master's degree on the subject of prostitution. Her major interests are in the areas of marriage and family counseling and human sexual behavior.

THE NEW MASSEUSE

Play for Pay

PAUL K. RASMUSSEN
LAUREN L. KUHN

MASSAGE PARLORS have become a common sight throughout America in the last several years. They began in the great metropolitan areas, especially in San Francisco, Los Angeles, and New York, and it is in these areas that they have come to full bloom. But they are also springing up in out-of-the-way cities throughout the country. During a recent visit with his in-laws in a midwest city, one of our research colleagues was slightly shocked to see a little red building nestled among all the government buildings downtown—with a big sign proclaiming "Joyous Massage." But the full shock came only when his in-laws showed him another little building, with a small sign proclaiming "Bon Vivante Massage" announcing complete services, including overnight lodging, all just blocks from his in-laws' home—and also showed him the circular the parlor had delivered to all nearby residents.

AUTHORS' NOTE: We wish to thank Professor Jack Douglas for his invaluable comments on an earlier version of this paper. Also, we would like to thank Carol Ann, Sue, and Jean, as well as Jerry and Sandy for their help with the research.

[11]

Western City, with a metropolitan population of one million and a core city population of half a million, has not been in the forefront of the massage parlor explosion. But it has kept pace with most of the nation and is far more representative of the nation than those cities in the vanguard. In the past four years the number of massage parlors has jumped from 3 to 150. Business is booming, with an ever-wider segment of the population discovering the pleasures of the "fine art of the massage." Doctors, lawyers, and dentists enjoy this new-found pastime as much as salesmen, clerks, and laborers. And the controversy over the parlors rages in the city and county meetings, in courtrooms, and in the mass media.

The controversy over massage parlors centers on the question of sex. Are the parlors health spas, as their owners and supporters claim in public pronouncements, or are they centers of prostitution, as the police and their political attackers proclaim? Each side has extensive arguments and facts to support their claims. The opponents point to the sometimes sexy ads—"Nights of Paris Massage—A Girl for Every Taste." They also point to the "sexual format" of the massage itself.

The basic pattern of the massage puts a male customer in a room alone with a female masseuse, both in some state of undress. This sets the stage for such attacks as: "I'll bet I know which stiff muscle gets the most attention"—a comment which stems from the belief that a man and a woman alone in a room, both semi-nude and both touching each other, "have gotta be sexually involved." On the other hand, the supporters point to the healthful aspects of massage. Moreover, there are a lot of men in Western City who, from their own experience, claim the parlors are "straight." This was the experience of a friend, who claimed: "I don't know what you've found out, but I went to the Devil's Den, hoping to get laid, and all I got was a straight massage—sex never came up, dammit." Media coverage and court cases further add to the controversy and public confusion. Most people in Western City really do not know whether sexual services are offered or not, and many figure it is an even chance. The police contend that the "obvious is true." As one very experienced vice-squad officer told us: "We've been able to find only five straight parlors in Western City and even those we're not sure about—the rest are all houses of prostitution."

Our initial approach to the parlors, which involved classic "negotiations of entree" as social researchers, turned up some beautiful and sometimes outraged denials. One male researcher spent two months at a parlor becoming good friends with all the women, but especially one masseuse named Launa. Their friendship grew very intimate and our researcher had every reason to believe he had established the trust and confidence necessary for an honest exchange of information. Since Launa was candid about other things in the parlor, it made sense to also accept her claim that the parlor, for the most part, was straight and they were playing off other parlors' reputations to get customers while staying out of trouble with the police. But there was also evidence to the contrary. Our researcher witnessed, on several occasions, a fifty-dollar bill finding its way into the woman's purse and another friend claimed he had been to the parlor and received sexual services.

We decided to adopt an insider, in-depth approach. Fortunately, the female researchers on our team were able to get to know some masseuses quite well informally. They told us how it was done and once we knew, we were able to use that information to obtain other facts. Subjects were less inhibited, and we discovered there are indeed basic and extensive changes taking place on the American sex scene.

THE SETTING

Generally, massage parlors reflect the area they are in and the clientele they serve. In downtown business districts, they are converted store fronts and cater mostly to the tastes of the nearby military personnel. In residential areas, they are remodeled homes with the gruff atmosphere of their working-class customers. In the suburbs, they are housed in the local shopping centers complete with the decor of the suburbanite bar. They generally are dimly lit inside with drapes drawn, but all have the bright neon light proclaiming "massage." Most have waiting rooms furnished with a couch, several chairs, and a desk. The rest of the parlor is subdivided into private rooms for massage and facilities for bathing. The private rooms have a massage table covered with sheets or towels, a chair to hang clothes, and a shelf stocked with oils, powders, and lotions. The bathing facilities include things such as a shower, bath tub, and sauna.

Layla's Massage is typical of most parlors. It is located in a small shopping center along with several other businesses and looks strangely out of place with its drapes drawn. It is certainly not the typical store front. In fact, you might assume that the place is closed, but upon closer inspection you see the "open" sign. As a masseuse, you might feel rather self-conscious as you approach the parlor. The man from the barber shop next door is peering at you with curiosity and the secretary in the real estate office is also checking you out. After all, they think they know what you do.

The bells on the door jangle loudly as you enter. The change in atmosphere is a little overwhelming. You have stepped from the bright sunlight and hustle bustle of the outside world to the quiet, dimly lit surroundings of the massage parlor. It takes a moment to adjust your eyes to the relative darkness. Before you see the couch, table, and the reception desk up front, you hear the stereo playing softly. The soft blue lighting, the current issues of *Playboy* and *Penthouse* on the table, the picture of a provocative woman on the wall, all blend to create a seductive, sensuous atmosphere. It takes awhile, but slowly the atmosphere begins to affect how you feel. You begin to think sexy and act sexy. Now you are ready for the day's work so you take your place behind the desk and wait for your first customer.

THE MASSEUSE'S ENTRY TO THE SCENE

Masseuses come from all walks of life. Their family backgrounds can range from the upper classes of society to the very lowest. Their ages range from eighteen to thirty. Their physical appearances vary also, from the very attractive to the average, but all the women are at least pleasant in appearance. Generally, the women have a liberal view of sex and have had an early exposure to sexual relations. Most have an ambiguous view of their personal social worth, and all need money. Like most members of Western City, they have a vague understanding about the sexual nature of the massage parlors and are willing, within limits, to perform certain sexual acts.

There are severe social constraints against becoming a masseuse. Unlike the customer, it is not possible for the masseuse to claim a "temporary loss of sanity" due to drinking too much or being pressured by "the boys." She is out there day after day, repeatedly exchanging sex for money. As a result, her choice of occupation says something about her "substantial self." As one masseuse put it: "At first, I couldn't look at myself as a prostitute, everyone knows that a prostitute is the lowest form of human existence. But then I just couldn't deny the facts, it was me out there, the real me out there, taking money for sex. I guess that's prostitution." This self-image as a prostitute must also be shared in many cases by close friends and intimates. This raises the obvious question, why would anyone choose such a profession?

Motives

It has always been a very common belief that women who choose to become prostitutes do so only as a last resort. This assumption was made in the early studies of prostitution (Parent-Duchatelet, 1837), by the different commission reports of the 1900s (Chicago Vice Commission, 1911; Kneeland, 1913), and by the more recent studies (Greenwald, 1958; Barlay, 1968). The prostitutes either lack the skills necessary to get other jobs, are so unattractive that no one would marry them, come from so low a social background that no one would want them, or they have been seduced into the profession not knowing what they were getting in to. In short, they have rather limited chances for success in life. Even those who seem to be "on the side of" the prostitute call for the banding together of the prostitutes to fight jointly their economically exploited circumstance (Verlade and Warlick, 1973). Our investigation of massage parlors strongly contradicts these views. In fact, quite the opposite is true.

The pay and the working conditions are very favorable. There are basically two common payment schedules for the masseuse. The first and most common is commission. The masseuse receives from 40% to 50% of the massage fee. The second is an hourly wage and ranges from $2-$3 an hour. In either case, she keeps all the money for sexual services. The cost of a straight half-hour massage ranges from $5-$15 and entails simply the masseuse massaging the customer. Variations on the basic massage include the topless or bottomless massage, the switch, where the customer massages the masseuse for part of the time, and the double massage where two women massage the customer. Each of these variations costs more, adding around $5 to the basic massage price.

The sexual services are called "extras" and are paid for in addition to the basic massage fee. Sexual services fall most commonly into three categories: (1) manual stimulation (locals, hand jobs) costing around $10, (2) oral sex (french, blow jobs) averaging $15, and (3) intercourse (lays, balling) ranging around $30. Variations of these types are sometimes offered and as with the massage increase the price. For example, manual or oral sex can be done bottomless or topless. On rare occasions customers desire and receive unusual sex such as anal intercourse (Greek), being urinated on (golden showers), or being tied (bondage).

In the course of one eight-hour shift, a masseuse will have anywhere between two and six customers, each earning her an average of $25. This breaks down to anywhere from $50 to $150 per day, or $12,000 to $36,000 per year. A good income is definitely an important motive for becoming a masseuse. As one university graduate masseuse put it:

If I could find a straight job that paid as well, I'd take it in a minute. But where can anyone just out of college find a job that pays twenty-four thousand dollars a year? Where could anyone find a job like that? It's good money and I enjoy it.

Even though some masseuses work only part-time they easily earn enough to live a good life.

Another important motive for becoming a masseuse is the "fast life" that is part of the business. By the fast life we mean the excitment and fun one experiences as part of the everyday existence on the job. The fast life cannot be any better explained than by a happily married masseuse:

I quit the parlor for six months or so. The police were really hassling the parlors then. But I couldn't stand the boredom—not having a purpose in life. Now I'm back, living in two worlds. At home, I sit and read with my husband. That's the routine part. I feel comfortable there, I've got my man and nobody is going to hassle me. I can go out to a bar and the men won't try to pick up on me. Other women don't see me as a threat. I've known him for a long time and we've been through a lot together. He puts up with the worst side of me—when I'm on the rag and a real bitch—when I'm super depressed and down on life. Times that I wouldn't want to lay on anyone else. But this life is so predictable, so stable, that it's taken all the fun out of sex. I mean, for me to really enjoy sex, there's got to be some mystery to it. I really get off making it with someone new. Learning what's in his head, overcoming all the new problems of getting it on in bed. It's really exciting doing something that just about everyone else thinks is wrong. What I really did is looking across the room catching someone's eye—instant turn on. It's like this guy who came into the parlor. He had a good body and his eyes, you could really tell that in his eyes he really wanted me. I climbed right up on the table and got it on—good straight fucking. And that's how it is. I live in my stable world, doing what's necessary to get by. And then I live the fast life for all the fun and excitement.

Not only do the masseuses make good money, but they also enjoy the life style that is associated with it. They have not been forced into the profession because they lacked the skills, appearance, or opportunity for another profession. They clearly have not been seduced into the business out of ignorance. This is not to say that there are no problems associated with the job.

Limits

Most women starting out in the business set limits on what sex they are willing to perform. Some women will just do hand jobs, others will do just hand jobs and blow jobs and still others will perform anything including lays. While there are exceptions, the general path progresses from hand jobs, to blow jobs, to lays. This progression is further reflected in the price structure. Lays are universally more expensive than the other types of sex. The limits imposed by the women also go further than just the type of sex. Some women will perform lays only with regular customers that they find particularly nice or attractive.

The purpose of setting limits is similar to that in our general society. It helps maintain a positive self-image as well as a positive evaluation of one's self by others. This point was made clear by the statement of one novice masseuse when she said: "I've just done hand jobs since the first day on the job. After all, I go to church and believe in God. There's really nothing wrong with locals, the penis is just another part of the male body and needs to be massaged too." Boyfriends or close intimates also find limits important, as the boyfriend of one masseuse put it: "I'm really glad Mary decided to stick to just BJ's. That doesn't bother me so much. We still have something that is just between us. I really don't think I could handle it if I knew that anyone with the right amount of money could have her."

MEANINGS OF SEX

Although limits set in the parlors function in much the same way as in our general society, they take a different path. From our numerous discussions with customers and with members of society in general, the progression in our society develops first with hand jobs, then to lays, and finally blow jobs. Further, customers in parlors overwhelmingly prefer oral sex. Using an economic model of supply and demand, one would expect BJs to be the most expensive. The general society sees oral sex as the extreme and even has laws against it. But BJs cost less than lays. So it appears that masseuses and customers disclosed several practical reasons for this. Customers claimed they liked BJs because they did not get them at home, and could lay back and enjoy the sensual variations possible with the human mouth; some mistakenly believed they could not contract venereal disease. Masseuses, on the other hand, pointed out the advantages of not having to undress, the economy of labor, and the increased ability to accommodate numerous men. Other possible explanations include the symbolic meanings attached to various body parts. The hand is the least intimate part of the body, often extended to strangers during the custom of "handshaking." The mouth is next, such as kissing a friend. And the most intimate part of the body is the genital region, commonly contacted by only the most intimate of lovers. This reasoning concurs with our findings of guilt neutralization: as long as one leaves the most intimate form of body contact to one's mate, one is not being unfaithful. All of these reasons come into play, so that oral sex is the most popular form of sex for masseuses and customers.

Breaking Limits

Whatever the reasons, limits are set by the women and as in our general society, men are always trying to seduce the women into breaking them. We found three ways this was commonly done. First, customers may ask for another masseuse who will do as he likes, or he may simply not return to the parlor. This prevents the woman from building up her clientele, a major source of her earnings and the major protection against police detection. One masseuse explained why she started doing BJs: "I'd been working here for about two weeks, and I just wasn't getting the money. The other girls were giving head and it didn't take the customers long to figure it out. I just sat there and watched all this money walk right out the door. So I figured if I was going to make it in this business I'd have to start giving BJ's." The second approach is more subtle. Customers would come in and become friends of the women. Another masseuse who started out with just hand jobs and later started giving BJs and lays explained how this happened:

> My boyfriend and I decided that I'd just do hand jobs, there was plenty of money with just that. But then I got to know a few of the guys really well. They'd take me out to lunch or just sit around the parlor and talk. After a while, I figured I'd ball these guys if they weren't in the parlor, so why not? But I really had to hide it from my boyfriend, he'd just shit if he knew.

The third way is open hostility from the customer. One masseuse who had maintained her limits described one time when it happened to her:

> The first thing I noticed when I walked in the room was his hat, he'd hung it over the light and the room was really dark. He'd signed up for a switch and wanted to massage me first. Right away he started getting really kissy. Then he said, "I bet you make love real good." When he found out he wasn't going to get laid, he got really pissed. He started swearing at me, put his clothes on, and left after he put his cigarette out in my coffee.

The pressures to conform to customer desires are especially strong and masseuses who stay in the business generally conform. While they may not break all limits, they generally must offer some form of sexual service. One veteran to the scene said:

When I first started working here I decided: absolutely no sex. I could give a good massage and that should be enough. Then came along my first customer. He had been in the hospital for two months without any sex and just wanted to get off. He had the scars and all, so I felt really sorry for him. I decided that I'd make an exception, just this once. Since then, I make a lot of exceptions—to the point that the exceptions have become the rule.

PROFESSIONALISM

It is common for a masseuse to assert that she is a professional. One reason for this is that she considers herself an expert in her field. Not in the art of massage, ironically, but in her ability to deal openly with sex and to cater to the specific sexual needs of her customers. As one masseuse put it: "I am definitely a professional here. I have a skill and the skill is sex. It's not like everyone else. I do sex in the parlor as a job, and I'm good at it. I know a lot of techniques and I practice them all the time. Most men tell me that I'm better than their wives or lovers."

Disinterest

An important aspect of professionalism is disinterest. By disinterest we mean that a masseuse is able to look at her job objectively and not become emotionally involved. Disinterest allows the masseuse to justify the fact that she is getting paid for sex. If she were really involved in sex with customers, it would be difficult to rationalize getting paid for it, and customers would no doubt wonder if they should be getting paid to satisfy her. However, there is a conflict of interest here because in many cases a man expects the masseuse to get involved to a certain degree and to enjoy him personally or to get turned on by him. His ego is at stake and he wants to feel that he is capable of sexually arousing a woman. And so at the risk of losing clientele because of her lack of emotion and interest, a masseuse is compelled to "get into it" to a certain extent; in other words, to fake it. In this case a masseuse might breathe harder, or moan a little, but not to the point of having an orgasm. Of course, she is probably often sincerely interested in a customer but there are always times when she must appear happier or friendlier or more interested than she feels, and also times when she is compelled to feign sexual excitation that she does not feel.

Occasionally, quite the opposite is true. Girls feign disinterest even though they are sexually aroused. As one masseuse said:

I had this nice old guy come in and he paid me $20.00 to perform oral sex on me. He said all he wanted was to make me feel good. He started off really slow which made me feel really at ease . . . he knew what he was doing . . . and then all of a sudden I got sexually aroused. I laid there on my back trying to control my breathing and stomach muscles, so he wouldn't know. After it was all over he asked me if I had gotten off. I told him no, but I did enjoy it.

What is important is that the involvement remains a pseudo-involvement; objectivity is essential. The problems that arise as a result of becoming involved are best illustrated in the case of Carla. Because she enjoyed sex, being a masseuse gave her an opportunity to do what she liked and to get paid well to do it. But liking one's work too much can present problems:

It just seems unfair to accept money for something that you enjoy. So when I do get off on a customer I really feel guilty about charging him. When I first started out, I didn't charge guys that I got off with. But it turned out that I wasn't making any money. I also got really emotionally involved with the customers. I just couldn't handle it. So I changed parlors and tried to remain aloof from the situation. When I do get off, I really try to hide it. I just don't think that's professional.

Play Acting

If a masseuse is professionally oriented and fairly perceptive, she will try to psych-out a customer's "type" as soon as he walks in the parlor. Masseuses become very adept at picking up clues about what kind of woman a customer will best respond to, i.e., does he try to develop a rapport with the masseuse, does he come on very sexually, does he like to be told what to do. Within a few minutes a masseuse can usually determine what "his type of woman" is and then cater to his particular needs by putting on her own performance. It is part of her professionalism. As one masseuse said: "When I walk out of that room, with my money in hand, you can't believe the feeling of success I have. Like, you know, a job well done. I know that I really made the guy happy and I was paid well to do it."

It might be added that this "act" aspect of the work is rarely discussed. It is extremely important for the man to feel that the situation is real. He wants to believe that the girl is not putting him on, even though, deep down inside, he might know that this is true. For the moment, he suspends the obvious and enjoys the pleasure of the performance.

INTERNAL DYNAMICS OF MASSAGE PARLORS

One nearly universal concern of people is the maintenance of a respectable concept of self. Most people want others to see them in a positive light and everyone wants to see themselves in a positive light. People develop a wide range of tests to evaluate their social worth. For example, success in sports demonstrates skills of the body, educational levels attained are taken as proof of intelligence, and leadership ability is evidence of personal charisma. These tests rank people, so that one either wins or loses in sports, has a degree or does not, is the leader or the one being led. There are certain restrictions placed on too much success. For example, if a person's chances are too slim to pass the test, he may simply withdraw from the test, try to change the ground rules of the particular test, or, in the extreme, resort to open violence. Further, people often band together and become part of a team, so that one's individual value is tied to that of the team. But regardless of whether it is a group or individual effort and regardless of the kinds of restrictions placed on the testing, the essence of the relationship is competition. You gain or lose a positive image of self at the profit or loss of others.

Competition is also an important aspect of the masseuse's job. They cannot rely on their occupational category for a respectable image. In fact, quite the opposite is true; the stigma of a masseuse is something to be overcome. The test for the masseuse revolves around the relative number of customers who choose her and the amount of money she can exact for her extras. By having more customers than other girls, she is able to claim a higher self-image. By receiving money for sex, she not only can compare her income with others, but also she can claim superiority to the customer.

Marketing Self

There are several techniques which the girls use to improve their chances of success. Perhaps the most difficult thing to manipulate is physical appearance. The *Playboy* centerfold has become the sexual ideal, and it is for this type of image that masseuses strive. Few women, if any, are born this way, and so they attempt to compensate for their deficiencies by wearing flattering clothes, choosing a becoming hairstyle, buying the appropriate make-up, and so on. Certainly the braless look can be very sexy, and the least amount of clothing a woman wears generally points in her favor when it is time for the customer to make a decision.

BODY LANGUAGE

The use of body language and seduction rhetoric is more easily manipulated than physical appearance, and does not require anything in terms of a money investment. Only time and a willingness to learn from others are needed. People are very conscious of body language, and masseuses use this knowledge to their advantage in their initial encounters with customers. If a masseuse is anxious to give a man a massage, she can easily communicate this through eye contact, body touching and body posture, relative body position, and body movement. In the case where one masseuse is more attractive than another, the latter may compensate by coming on strong with her body language, and this type of presentation of self makes her more desirable to the potential customer than even a more attractive woman.

SEDUCTION RHETORIC

Seduction rhetoric is also used by masseuses. For example, a masseuse might be sitting in a chair with a pose that appears to be very casual but is actually well planned, give a customer "the look," and say, "You know, I could give you a r-e-a-l-l-y good massage." The implication is clear here; the customer is being assured that he will get sex once he signs up for a massage.

Both body language and seduction rhetoric are marketing techniques that are used primarily in the reception room before the massage has begun. It can really be to a woman's advantage to get a new customer first, as many men will return to the same masseuse provided they like her. Once the massage has begun, however, there are other marketing techniques that may be used to make one masseuse more desirable than another. As indicated, some women specialize in lays and locals and no frenches, or just locals and frenches, or just locals. One masseuse who decided to do only locals was competing with other women who offered a broader range of sexual services. Consequently, in order to build up a clientele, she had to market herself and her hand jobs very well. She accomplished this in two ways. Rather than standing next to the customer and masturbating him, which is the more common position, she completely undressed and sat on the man's stomach, facing his penis. Then she came up with the idea of a "Hopi Indian ball massage." She would lightly massage the balls of her customer with oil before giving him the local. In other words, she spent a lot of time and imagination in dealing with her customers. She also described the procedure to the customer ahead of time, which titillated his sense of the exotic or bizarre, and in addition it allowed the masseuse to charge more than the regular $5-$10 for a hand job.

However, a customer usually comes to a parlor with a particular sex act in mind, and a masseuse who is willing to accommodate his desires will generally have more customers than the girl who specializes. It is no less true in parlors than in general business that it is a good policy to please your customers. This takes on greater significance when the parlors are located in areas which are dependent upon return clientele.

All of these marketing techniques are employed by the general public to some extent. Although people might not be selling themselves directly, in a subtle way they are marketing themselves continually in various social situations. The major difference is that while in general society marketing takes place over a prolonged period of social interaction, in parlors it is generally a "one-shot deal." Because marketing in parlors occurs over a briefer period of time, it is necessarily more overt and less subtle than marketing that takes place in social situations. How a woman markets herself, in a massage parlor or the society at large, is largely dependent upon her own individual taste; and this is a product of social and class origin. You can find a masseuse who is reminiscent of the hard-core hooker stereotype just as easily as you can find a woman who presents herself in a tasteful, sophisticated manner.

Rate Busting

As in general society, there are problems in marketing oneself too well. In massage parlors, this problem presents itself in the form of the "rate-buster." As stated earlier, to a large extent masseuses establish their personal worth by their relative success. This structures their relationships to each other as a competitive one. For one masseuse to be successful, it is necessary that another masseuse be less successful. This necessity is generated by the fact that women are competing for the same rewards. Rate-busters are women who manage marketing too well and they end up getting more than their share of customers. Understandably, other masseuses resent rate-busters and consequently they must find some way in which to deal with them. In our research, we found several common ways of doing this.

RUMORS

In the event the woman is new, and has not secured her position in the parlor, unfavorable rumors can be circulated that threaten her job standing. The kinds of rumors range from stealing money, breaking house rules of behavior, using drugs, getting arrested, and spreading disease. Linda, an extremely attractive and a rather well-educated woman, had just been hired and was assigned to work several shifts with Lee, a reasonably attractive woman who had been doing well in the business. However, many of Lee's customers became interested in Linda and started seeing her. At this time, Lee went to the boss and complained that Linda was not "checking customers out" sufficiently and her actions were setting the parlor up for an eventual "bust." In addition, Lee claimed that Linda was cold and unfriendly toward customers, and therefore discouraged business. Because Lee had been working at the parlor much longer than Linda had, the boss tended to take her word over Linda's. It was necessary for Linda to gain support from girls of other shifts to deal with Lee's harassment.

BEATING THEM AT THEIR OWN GAME

A second way in which rate-busters are dealt with is to beat them at their own game. If women are finding it difficult to compete, they might react by attempting to redo their image, i.e., wear sexier clothes, try a new hairdo, have better come-ons, or whatever.

PRICE CUTTING

However, the most common way to deal with rate-busters is to undercut them in price. For example, if a rate-buster charges $30 for a lay, another woman might start charging $15 or $20, and as a result, she would get more business. An illustration of this is the case of Sandy, a masseuse who was rather overweight and generally not very attractive, but was rather well endowed. It was probably on this basis that she was able to get customers at all. She began doing lays for $10 or $15, which was considerably under the going rate of $30. All of a sudden, Sandy began getting a lot of business. Customers would start coming in and requesting Sandy all of the time while the other, better-looking girls sat around and wondered what was happening. In time, customers began complaining to the other masseuses that they were charging too much: "Why should I pay you thirty dollars when Sandy will do a lay for ten?" What happened was that now Sandy herself had in fact become the rate-buster, and now it was up to the other masseuses to deal with the problem of her getting more business. In this case, they did this by complaining to the boss, who consequently put pressure on Sandy to charge the going rate unless she wanted to lose her job. When Sandy complied, she was still in the same predicament of not being able to compete. Eventually she quit the job.

OSTRACISM

Obviously, there are some problems in trying to beat the competition. There is definitely a strain between competition and cooperation. Prices are not only determined by what people will pay, but also by what people will ask. In the massage parlor situation it is in the interest of all the girls involved to cooperate and to organize the prices set for extras. While everyone as a general rule will act in her own interest, in this case it benefits individual interest to act in the group's interest. If rate-busting were to go unchecked, the end result would be chaos. Masseuses would not end up making any money, and a great deal of hostility and resentment would be generated in the group.

The last way to deal with rate-busters is socially to ostracize them. This is done, not only in terms of the work setting in the parlor, but also outside in social settings. Social pressure is a common technique found in regular society; it is not unique to the parlor. For example, by refusing to talk or interact with another person, or by acting very critical and sarcastic, one can make another individual feel extremely frustrated and uncomfortable. Sherry was a girl who received this treatment as a result of the tremendous business she did. This might not have been so bad in itself, but she had a tendency to flaunt it, i.e., telling everyone how many "requests" she had had that evening, bragging about the amount of money she had made, and so on. Her coworkers reacted negatively to this, and before long she was either given the "silent treatment," criticized openly, or talked about behind her back.

The Threat of Arrest

One of the greatest occupational hazards that a masseuse must deal with is getting arrested. There are several ways in which a girl is likely to be busted. By far the most common way is for a vice-squad officer to pose as an undercover agent and handle the arrest himself. The law governing prostitution is California State Penal Code 647(a) and (b), which covers solicitation and the commission of a lewd act. There are several lines of defense that a masseuse may adopt to protect herself from being arrested on either or these charges. One is to be able to detect that a customer is a vice-squad officer by means of a "checking-out procedure."

CHECKING OUT

Some of the techniques for detection are very intangible. A woman must rely heavily on her sense of perception and intuition in checking out customers. From the moment that a customer walks in the door, the masseuse picks up clues that allow her to determine whether or not the guy might be a cop. First of all, she will probably categorize the customer according to a certain type; she will pick up on whether he is obviously in the military, a businessman, a salesman, a young surfer type, or whatever. Within each of these categories is the possibility that the man is a vice-squad officer in disguise. More specifically, a masseuse will check out a guy's haircut (is the guy's hair short, but not short enough to be in the military, is he a long-hair?); clothing (is he wearing a work uniform or a suit or faded jeans and T-shirt?); mannerisms (how he carries himself—is he confident or rather shy?); language (does he use jargon that is unique to his apparent occupation, how articulate is the customer given the vernacular he should know?).

In addition to his general appearance, there are other characteristics that a masseuse looks for in checking out her customers. Some customers come in and appear to be quite nervous. This may be indicative of a man's genuine uneasiness because this is his first visit to a parlor, or it may be the kind of nervousness that a person displays when he is trying to cover up something; or it may be the kind of nervousness that is brought on by being sexually aroused. Masseuses must also be wary of customers who attempt to develop rapport with them right away. They learn to distinguish between the guy who is just being friendly or the guy who is just an obnoxious nuisance, or the guy who is really trying to glean some inside information about the masseuse or the parlor. Again, exactly how the women do this is largely dependent upon their intelligence and perception. A masseuse who is alert and aware will do a much better job of screening a potential customer than the girl who is disinterested or spaced out.

Another clue that arouses a masseuse's suspicion is if the customer inquires if extras are available and he does so right out at the front desk. This can mean one of two things: the guy is not familiar with the massage parlor scene and so he does not "know" that extras are to be discussed with the individual masseuse in the massage room; or, the guy is a vice-squad officer or an informer who is trying to set up the parlor. Most massage parlor owners insist that masseuses always claim that the place is straight when asked over the phone or at the desk. However, for the guys who are genuine customers this is a bad deal. They will probably leave and never come back unless they learn the inside line from a friend. For this reason, a masseuse may insinuate that extras are available or she may come right out and say it. As a general rule, however, masseuses are concerned enough about their own welfare that they will not do this, even though it means losing a few customers now and then.

Masseuses are also suspicious of men who come in the parlor in twos. Vice-squad officers have a habit of doing this, and it is the ideal situation for them. This way there are two people to testify against the masseuse in court. It is generally a good idea not to do extras with men that come in the parlor in twos, especially if there are only two masseuses working. Once the massage is paid for, a man may ask for a receipt. If he does, this also arouses suspicion. Most men are not interested in carrying a massage receipt in their pockets as evidence of their visit, and as massages are not tax deductible, there is no logical reason to keep it—unless, of course, you are an undercover agent, and in that case you might choose to keep it. From the moment that the man walks in the door until he has paid for his massage, the perceptive masseuse will pick up all of the clues we have mentioned and then she will form an overall impression. This checking-out procedure continues as the masseuse leads her customer down the hall to his room. During this time she may inquire, "Have you been here before?" and if the answer is yes, she may press him later for information regarding which masseuse he had, and so on. In order not to arouse suspicion by asking this question, a masseuse may comment in response to the man's answer, "Oh, then you know where the bathroom and shower are?" At this point the masseuse shows the customer to his room, instructs him to undress and lie on the table, and says that she will be back shortly. She gives him enough time to undress and then returns to the room.

Upon entering the room, the masseuse continues with her checking-out procedure. The first thing she notices is the man's body position: is he lying face down or face up; is he completely naked or partially clothed; is he using a towel to cover his genitalia; is he lying on the table in a relaxed position, seemingly ready for the massage or is he sitting on the table looking like he is ready to talk. The masseuse takes all of these things into account in the first couple of seconds that she enters the room.

If the man appears to be relatively passive, the masseuse will initiate the conversation. This is to her advantage: she can control everything that is said and done during the course of the massage. She may begin by greeting him, asking him if he prefers lotion, powder, oil, or alcohol. As she begins to massage, she will ask him a series of questions that, on the surface, appear to be nothing more than friendly interest. These questions are all calculated to give the masseuse a clearer picture of the customer's background and interests. She will inquire about the man's job, his family, where he lives, and what he does in his spare time. She will ask if he gets massages often, or how he found out about this particular parlor, or what other parlors he has frequented. She will always be looking for consistencies and inconsistencies in his "story"; i.e., if the man claims that he is a local construction worker, are his hands rough and calloused? If he is a salesman, can he discuss marketability of his product with specific knowledge of other competive products? By this time, the masseuse has a very definite feeling about the customer; whether he is "cool" (not an undercover agent), or whether many of the things he has said do not check out and he is "weird." It is this positive or negative evaluation which determines the willingness of the masseuse to engage in sex. If he is weird he will receive a straight massage and nothing more. If he is cool and knows how to play the game, he will have his sexual desires fulfilled.

The Word Game

Another important technique used to protect the masseuse from legal constraint is the word game. The effectiveness of the word game is derived from the nature of the laws against prostitution and, ironically, also from the moral attitudes of our society. A prostitute is guilty of breaking the law if she either (1) solicits her customer, i.e., asks him if he would like to pay for her services or, (2) commits a lewd act, i.e., takes part in a sex act. The purpose of the word game is for the masseuse to get the customer to solicit her for the sex act, thus freeing her from prosecution under solicitation. In order for one to be guilty of committing a lewd act, an actual sex act must occur and since it takes "two to tango" this means the vice officer would have to take part also in the sex act. While this is within the limits of the law, as a "feigning accomplice," it is generally not within the moral limits of our society. Hence, the moral codes of our society themselves prevent enforcement.

There are several methods a masseuse can use to get the customer to solicit her. The massage itself is sometimes enough, with the erotic finger tip massage coming close and sometimes touching erogenous zones of the body. Other techniques include "Take my hands and place them where you want me to massage" or "Our time is almost up, is there anyplace *else* you would like massaged?" Other innovative techniques are sometimes added, such as asking if he is in any way connected with the law enforcement agency, what identification he can produce to prove who he really is, the actual signing of a statement to the effect that he solicited her, and the taping of the whole conversation to be used in court if necessary. But, generally, the masseuse has little trouble getting the customer to solicit her, the slightest sign of sexual interest is usually enough. A typical solicitation would be:

L: Do you give extras?

M: What do you mean by extras?

L: Like give head or things like that?

M: Are you soliciting me?

L: Well, yes.

M: Ya, I do, but it's really expensive now.

L: How about $20.00?

M: Yes.

Law Enforcement

Arrests that have been made regardless of the word game and checking-out procedures are generally the result of a girl too new to the scene or a vice officer who is not aware of the legal restrictions placed on his behavior. One such case, involving Cheri, resulted from a little of each circumstance. Cheri was arrested the first day on the job for soliciting a hand job. Since it was her first day she lacked the skills to sense the presence of a vice-squad officer. On the other hand, the vice-squad officer, not understanding the nature of the law, played the word game and made the solicitation, not only once, but many times. The case went to trial by judge and was dismissed immediately on the sole testimony of the arresting officer. The grounds for the dismissal were: (1) no act of solicitation was made by the masseuse, hence no infraction of 647(b) and, (2) no lewd act had occurred—647(a). While the case was dismissed, it was not without great personal loss to Cheri. She still had to pay $1,000 to a lawyer, to spend many hours in court, and to live with a certain amount of emotional strain.

The conviction rate for arrests involving prostitution is extremely low. Cases are either plea bargained to the lessor offense of disturbing the peace or thrown out of court altogether. So, except for some harassment by police, massage parlor sex-for-money becomes quasi-legal.

CONCLUSION

Traditional theories of prostitution have taken the functional view (Merton, 1938) that prostitutes have internalized the values (ends) of society but lack the legitimate means to achieve them. For example, the prostitute values the financial rewards of our society but lacks the education or job skills necessary to achieve them. She turns to prostitution as the last resort. The women become exploited by the pimps, owners, and customers (Verlarde and Warlick, 1973) which leads to deep emotional problems such as low self-esteem (Greenwald, 1958).

Many findings in this article conflict with these traditional theories. Part of these differences can be attributed to basic attitudinal changes in our society. The liberation movements of both women and homosexuals, the acceptance of public nudity, and sexual freedom, all carry the same message: "The body is a source of pleasure and should be used for pleasure." While all members of society have not endorsed this new attitude, its impact is evident in the increased sexual nature of entertainment and the explosion of public nudity on the stages, the beaches, and in many other places. Clearly, this new attitude is very different from that of the past: "save yourself until you're married." The effect on prostitution is obvious. Now a girl can say: "I'm only doing what I like, and if someone wants to pay me for it, that's great. I can use the money."

The massage parlor front is equally important. By playing the word game and checking out each customer, prostitutes have a quasi-legal status. The masseuses are simply giving a massage, and if one should ask for sexual pleasure, he not she, is breaking the law. Furthermore, the massage parlor front gives the masseuses freedom of choice. If a customer comes in whom the women do not like, for whatever reason, they can give him nothing more than a straight massage. This allows the masseuse to maintain her self-respect. As one masseuse put it: "I'm not a common prostitute, I only do those customers that I especially like." This also fits with new American sex values: "If it feels good, do it; at least if you really like the other person."

The changes in society's attitudes and the existence of the massage parlor front have interested a new type of employee in prostitution. While other forms of prostitution have been dominated by girls from lower-class origins, the new masseuse is typically a middle-class girl with some college education. To some degree, then, the differences in our findings can be explained by the fact that massage parlor sex is really different than traditional forms of prostitution. The existence of this new middle-class masseuse seriously questions the assumed causal relationship between prostitution and social pathological behavior (Greenwald, 1958). The "sick" behavior which has been reported seems to be a product of a lower-class background and the life styles common to this class.

We feel the major source of this traditional bias is the methods which have been used to study prostitution. Most of the studies which have been done on prostitution focus on the lower-class prostitute who is in jail. Similarly, the subject matter of sexual behavior creates intense emotional conflict in all those associated with it. Since there is conflict, it is difficult not to take sides. If you are a male, you become either a customer or a boyfriend; and if you are a female, you become either straight or "in the business." Each of these roles limits the type of information you receive. Hence, it is important to have researchers playing each role to get all sides. As mentioned at the beginning of this paper, it took a female "insider-informant" to break through the straight front presented to our male researcher. There were many other incidences where the method of team field research allowed us to go beyond our sole reliance on the member's accounts. In many cases, we were able to match our own individual experiences and feelings against those given by members. In other cases, we spent the time necessary to break through the member's deceptions. Without exception, we have all felt it impossible to gain an in-depth understanding without the benefit of the diverse characteristics and information of a team.

Finally, returning to the question which concerned us in the beginning, we have found that there is indeed a basic change taking place within American society over the social forms of sex-for-money. There are at least a few other studies of massage parlors that are reliable in some degree, although in all cases we have found that they were "fronted-out" in some important ways by failing to use women who could deal with the inside informants as friends. These have revealed the same basic pattern as our findings. Obviously, there may be some important differences in what goes on behind the parlor fronts from one part of the country to another, but the burden of proof now rests with those who contend that these are not fronts for sex-for-money acts. We expect that, as the evidence accumulates around the country, it will be clear that America now has complex forms of quasi-legalized forms of sex-for-money and they are on a large and growing scale. We suspect this quasi-legal form is a half-way form, something less than legal because of continuing opposition to sex-for-money, but something more legal than prostitution has been in our society. This ambivalent situation is made possible by changing social feelings and values about sex. While past experience shows the hazards of predicting social events, we would predict these new forms of sex-for-money, carried out discreetly and perhaps with controlled hygienic conditions will become fully decriminalized in the years ahead.

REFERENCES

BARLAY, S. (1968) Sex Slavery. London: Heinemann.

Chicago Vice Commission (1911) The Social Evil in Chicago. Chicago: Gunthorp-Warren.

DAVIS, K. (1955) "Prostitution," in R. Merton and R. Nisbet (eds.) Social Problems. New York: Harcourt Brace & World.

GREENWALD, H. (1958) The Call Girl. New York: Ballantine Books.

KNEELAND, G. (1913) Commercialized Prostitution in New York City. Montclair, N.J.: Patterson Smith.

MERTON, R. (1938) "Social structure and anomie." Amer. Soc. Rev. (October).

PARENT-DUCHATELET, A.J.B. (1837) Prostitution Dans la Ville de Paris. 2 vols. Paris: J. B. Bailiere.

VERLARDE, A. and M. WARLICK (1973) "Massage parlors: the sensuality business." Society (December).

JERALD W. CLOYD is Assistant Professor of Sociology at the State University of New York, College at Geneseo. He is interested in sociological theory, urban sociology, and sociology of law, and he is currently doing research on urban legal problems.

THE MARKET-PLACE BAR

The Interrelation Between Sex,

Situation, and Strategies in the

Pairing Ritual of Homo Ludens

JERALD W. CLOYD

ALTHOUGH HETEROSEXUAL PAIRING can take place in a number of different environments, the "market-place bar" is especially structured to facilitate such encounters.[1] By market-place bar is meant a bar that caters specifically to young and usually single persons interested in meeting and possibly having sexual encounters with persons of a similar orientation. Many aspects of this analysis might also be applicable to homosexual bars, but the scope and data base of this paper are confined to heterosexual encounters. More specifically, the analysis will elucidate some of the interrelationships between: (1) the physical structuring of the bar to maximize members' discretionary powers to initiate and control encounters, (2) the typical motives and forms of presenting a marketable self within this physical structure, and (3) the typical structure through which such encounters evolve during the course of an evening.

Much barroom behavior seems disjointed and confused, with loud music in the background, possibly some members dancing, and many individuals making numerous and often fleeting contacts with others. However, there is a typical structure of motives and behavior that identifies the market-place bar. Specifically, members frequent such bars in an effort to find some "action," which in this sense refers to competition among members for perceived scarce resources in an environment that permits a minimum of personal control over the situation (Goffman, 1967: 149-269). Action within a market-place bar usually involves a concerted attempt by members to generate some form of social encounter, whether it is just to "meet some new people," to "score" (have a sexual encounter), or to meet a potential spouse.

The degree to which the individual is successful in such endeavors is often a function of experience within this type of situation. It will be shown that experienced members tend to generate a "presentation of self" (Goffman, 1959) that exhibits those qualities valued by members of the specific barroom situation (marketability)[2] and a level of control over the situation that is conducive to attaining his/her personal goals (obtaining friendship, sex, and/or a spouse). Although the specific style of presentation will differ between individuals, the typical structure of the bar, motives for being there, and the evolutionary structure of the encounter are similar. The more a member has gained an understanding of the typical structure of encounters within the barroom situation, the more "self-confidence" he or she usually exhibits. Experienced members tend to see the market-place bar as an area of increased discretionary power to initiate, negotiate, and possibly consummate an encounter with the opposite sex. The generally dark environment, intensity of sporadic sensory stimuli (e.g., loud music, flashing lights, and such), and a more open and relaxed feeling produced by the ingestion of alcohol facilitate a member's ability to generate an encounter. Experienced members use this milieu, and organize their behavior in ways that will fulfill their specific goals.

Members tend to gain experience, and hence self-confidence, through conversations with more experienced members, personal trial and error, and imitating others' behavior. Most novices frequent market-place bars in groups of two or more, to ensure some emotional support in case of difficulty in generating an encounter and to share information regarding interpersonal tactics and experiences. Specifically, both female and male members consult their friends in "sizing up" a member of the opposite sex, determining the best approach in initiating an encounter, and evaluating the probable success of a particular line of action. Once a general consensus has been reached it is incumbent on the individual to "make a move." This move consists of a series of trial-and-error interactions in which members become aware of the most successful lines of action in various situations. Members who have had considerable experience in these endeavors are seen as "smooth" and highly self-confident in their approach. The major portion of this paper is concerned with the tactics that are typically used to generate these encounters.

Finally, members gain self-confidence through imitating the behavior of other members who seem to be highly successful in generating encounters. This is especially true in the areas of styles of dress and dancing. Experienced members are sensitive to the fact that these styles are in constant flux and differ between particular bars, and hence will often practice a new dance step and groom themselves in the latest fashion at home. By practicing one's presentation prior to actually entering the barroom situation, the person generates a level of self-confidence and positive self-concept that is more easily maintained within the barroom situation.

Although members gain self-confidence in similar ways, typical motives or goals differ somewhat between males and females. Traditionally, males are socialized into being more aggressive in initiating encounters, and feel it is incumbent on them to initiate a conversation, to offer a female a drink, and/or to ask a female to dance. The male often initiates an encounter with a specific goal in mind, usually to have a sexual encounter, to score. The more experienced male often has a general idea of which females are most likely to be receptive for this type of encounter and will tend to pursue them. Specifically, women who exhibit intense eye contact, revealing clothes, and/or particularly sensuous body language are understood to be more open to an encounter and possible sexual relations.

Females, being socialized into a more passive role, can either wait for a male's initiation, or manifest a "come on" behavior to motivate specific males to generate an encounter. Come on behavior consists of the subtle indication that one is open to an encounter without actually initiating it oneself. Here again, eye contact is the predominant form of interaction. As the male "cruises" the bar and "checks out" (observes) the available females, a woman attempts to catch the male's eye and hold the eye contact for a longer than usual period of time. This form of interaction enables the female to make her intentions known and possibly motivate the male to initiate an encounter, without actually taking the risk of overtly initiating the encounter herself and being rejected. Hence, although males are required to take the initiative, there are specific behaviors open to females to attract a male.

Not only are the roles of males and females dissimilar, but the typical motives are often different. Traditionally, males are socialized into the idea that the culmination of a sexual encounter is a reflection of their masculinity and sexual attractiveness. Females, on the other hand, tend to be socialized into the notion that a sexual encounter should be interwoven with strong emotional and affective ties between the partners. Thus females are usually less interested in having a sexual encounter unless there has been considerable interaction, and an emotional bond has been established. Hence barroom behavior is usually characterized by an asymmetrical goal orientation between the sexes, with the female interested in getting to know the male per se, and the male getting to know the female in order to score.

Given the divergence in typical goals, the lines of action of males and females tend also to be different. Specifically, an experienced male will tend to focus on information indicating the general sexual intentions of a female, that is, whether she is married, attached to another male, tends to get sexually involved on the first night, and/or is interested in or attracted to him. The experienced female often focuses on whether a male is the kind of person with which she would be interested in having a significant relationship, that is, his socioeconomic status, whether he handles himself well in public, and/or the likelihood of his being interested in an emotional form of attachment.

METHODS AND DATA

The data for this paper consist of information that this author has gained through participant observation in 11 bars within a Western metropolitan area. These observations are supplemented by studies done by students from a local community college and a state university. A total of 27 students have made at least 1 observation of each of these bars; their findings have been the subject of discussion within a seminar situation led by this author. Generally, researchers have tended to take a "complete participant" (Gold, 1958) stance within these bars in an effort to become intimately aware of the typical mode of members' interaction. In this stance "a field worker takes a pretended role [i.e., that of barroom participant here] which fosters a heightened sense of self-awareness and an introspective attitude, because of the sheer necessity of indicating continually to himself that certain experiences are merely part of playing a pretended role" (Gold, 1958: 221).

Research in the market-place bar necessitated complete participation for a number of reasons. First, the large amount of noise and diversity of interaction required observers actually to engage other members in an encounter as opposed to just observing them. Second, researchers could not openly indicate that they were engaged in interaction primarily for sociological reasons, since this stance might seriously undermine others' interest in interacting.

A salient aspect of barroom behavior is the determination whether the alter is interested in a potentially sexual relationship. Therefore, if the researcher is understood to be interacting for some other reason (e.g., sociological study), then interest in continuing the interaction is lessened. Finally, many of the researchers have had past experience within the market-place bar situation and have developed considerable interpersonal skill in this type of environment. By engaging in actual participation in a number of encounters, researchers learned to reflect on their actions and to make conscious numerous tactics that they had simply taken for granted in the past. Hence, another source of data consists of the reflections made by participating researchers.

THE PHYSICAL STRUCTURE OF THE MARKET-PLACE BAR: THE USES OF PROPS TO GENERATE ENCOUNTERS

The barroom situation is physically structured into relatively defined areas of specialized activity. Most market-place bars have a bar, tables and chairs, a dance floor, an area in which a band plays, restrooms, and possibly a juke box and/or game area (such as pinball). The ways in which these areas are used are often differentiated according to sex. Females usually come in groups of two or more and head straight for a table and sit down, most often without checking out or cruising the place very much. They usually stick pretty close to those they came with and only start to check out the guys after they have staked out some territory (table). Males, on the other hand, given their more predatory role, will usually manifest more cruising behavior by more blatantly checking out the situation. This is usually done by walking around the entire barroom area and noting the different females and the degree to which their presence is acknowledged by the females, determining the likelihood of a potential encounter. After the place has been checked out, they will usually stake out some territory, often at the bar or some area in which there is a good visual access to those females who seem to be "available." The bar affords a particularly good visual vantage point given that the bar stools are usually a foot or so higher than the normal lounge chairs. If the place is crowded, males will often stake out some standing territory in a corner or near the dance floor so that access to females sitting or dancing is increased. Hence, males usually set themselves up in areas that afford the best view of those to be hustled, while females generally stake out territory at the conventional tables.

While the bar and tables are specialized areas for staking out territories, the restroom is often a specialized area for generating camaraderie. Ostensibly, the restroom is an area for relieving biological functions, but it also acts as a place to reorganize a member's show (comb hair, put on make-up, and so on), and to create levels of camaraderie with peers prior to the engaging of an adversary (member of the opposite sex). This is particularly true of males, who will make numerous statements such as "Did you see that blonde, would I like to get into some of that!" to other males while lined up at the urinals. In a similar manner, should a member be in a more negative mood due to a lack of contact with members of the opposite sex, the restroom can act as a place of consolation from other members of the same sex. Such statements occur like "Jesus, the band stinks, I can't get it on in this dump" or "The girls are really stuck-up here, you know of any places that really swing?" Such statements, of course, function to place the blame for failure on the general milieu and to decrease feelings of personal inadequacy. In either event, the restroom can be seen to have both a biological and a social function.

Other specialized territories may include the dance floor and gaming areas. The dance floor is usually the center of attraction and can be used by both males and females to increase the possibility of generating a successful encounter. Obviously, the dance floor is used as a means of initiating heterosexual contact when a male asks a female to dance, but there are uses beyond this. Often males will tend to crowd around the edge of the dance floor to watch for a particularly "sexy" dancer who does not seem to be too attached to her dance partner. A less aggressive male will determine the availability of a female by watching the success of other males asking her to dance; if she dances with several males and the initial ice is broken, he will make his move. Once a female is dancing, a male will often attempt to catch her eye and if the contact is maintained for a sufficiently long period, he may feel emboldened to ask her for the next dance. By watching a girl dance prior to initiating an encounter, a male will be able to determine whether she is possibly interested in him, and/or whether she is sexy when dancing. As one male patron put it:

> A lot of guys come here and bust their balls trying to get a girl to dance. I'd rather play it cool and be sure she's interested before I make a move. It's smarter to just lay back and watch them dance and make the rounds. If they're interested in you, they'll give you the eye or let you know they want to be hit on [have the male initiate an encounter]. Otherwise, why work up a sweat?

If the dance floor can function as a source of information for male tactics, it seems to act also as an arena of display for females. The female, when asked to dance by a stranger, will not look in his direction while dancing, at least initially. Often females will concentrate on dancing with a dead-pan expression or will focus on the other available males watching her. This disengagement display serves to maintain some territorial integrity in a situation that tends to reduce such integrity. Ostensibly, she is his partner while dancing, but given that the male usually initiates the encounter, she usually is not sure how she feels about the situation. Given this, the female will often act somewhat aloof and check out the guy with her peripheral vision or while he is not looking. It is often the case that she will have to make a tactical decision at the end of the dance. If she is interested in him, she will stay on the dance floor and attempt to generate a conversation or to give him some positive reinforcement (such as a smile) as they return to their places. However, this shift toward openness, if it occurs, is usually after the first dance. Hence, the dance floor can be a source of information for the male, and can be a source of conscious evaluation for the female.

The gaming area (in which pinball, pool, and shuffleboard are played) often acts as the center of attraction when the band or juke box are not playing and people are not dancing. While the band is on its break there is usually a marked shift toward the gaming area with males displaying their prowess and expertise in these areas. This area serves to maintain a sense of action and can be the source of conversation between bystanders. It is common for members to initiate conversations focusing on a particular game, a practice that gives a common focus of attention and facilitates the intersubjectivity necessary to maintain an encounter. Here, games act as just one source or focal point for the solution to the problem of generating intersubjectivity or a mutual attempt to create an interaction—a crucial aspect of the encounter.

THE PRESENTATION OF SELF: THE IMPORTANCE OF SELF-CONFIDENCE, KNOWLEDGE, AND LUCK

As indicated in the foregoing section of this analysis, the barroom situation is structured to maximize a member's potential freedom to initiate, construct, and possibly consummate an encounter with a member of the opposite sex. However, the effectiveness of a member's use of the barroom's specialized areas and relaxed normative structure hinges on the individual's understanding of how to manipulate these aspects of the situation to her or his own advantage. Generally, an individual who has a working knowledge of the more effective ways to do this is seen to have self-confidence. As one woman put it:

> Some guys just seem to know what they are doing. They know how to approach you, to talk to you, and just make you feel good. Then you get these nurds [socially incompetent individuals] who can't get anything right. They come on strong at first, but can't keep it together. The things they talk about, usually themselves, bore me; they just hang around until you dump them by going to the restroom or over to a friend to talk.

Self-confidence seems to involve an intuitive or cognitive understanding of the best ways to present the more "marketable" aspects of one's personality.

In this paper, self-confidence means that the individual manifests those attributes most valued by members of the social situation and presents them in a controlled, yet seemingly "natural" manner. Individuals who regularly frequent bars indicate that they develop through experience a level of understanding or knowledge of how to present themselves in the best manner possible. Members learn to "present a good line" or "get their show together" when they are seriously attempting to generate an encounter. One woman mentioned that "at first I used to just go out and play things as they came. After a while though, you get to know what kind of guys are going to give you what kind of line. I guess I can draw the guys I'm interested in to me and keep the creeps away if I want to."

A second aspect relating to self-confidence involves a member's ability to display and exchange those attributes most valued by members of the social situation. Within the market-place bar setting, sexual attractiveness and the display of these attributes is the predominant focus of attention for both males and females. Although sex may be a major aspect of the setting, other interests are often interrelated. As Schutz noted, "There is no such thing as an isolated interest. Interests have from the outset the character of being interrelated with other interest systems" (1970: 149). These other interests include the possibility of finding a permanent mate, attempting to gain positive reinforcement of one's sexual attractiveness, and simply finding some entertainment for the evening. The ways in which these different interests interrelate and affect the barroom interaction are complex and problematic. A member may go with the idea of just having a good time (entertainment) and meeting a future spouse; or he or she can be looking for a spouse and find that the encounter lasts only until morning.

There are several ways in which the more self-confident members consciously attempt to manipulate the situation in order to maximize the possibility of fulfilling their particular interests. Basically, the encounter passes through three stages: (1) the initiation of the encounter, (2) the negotiation, and (3) the final disclosures and/or exchange of rewards. Again, the ephemeral nature of barroom activity means that many initiations will not pass through to the final stages, and members may maintain several encounters simultaneously. However, it is possible to structure analytically an encounter into these stages and to delineate the ways members present themselves in each stage.

The Initiation of an Encounter

Of course, the different sex roles of men and women necessitate a different modus operandi for each in initiating an encounter. Essentially, both attempt to initiate an encounter by manifesting those features most valued within the particular social context. Women usually market sexual attractiveness by their choice of clothes, body language, and eye contact. The more provocative the clothing and body language, the more intense is the interaction during negotiations. Sometimes an experienced male studies a very sensually dressed female to determine whether he is "up to the interaction" or not. Often a strong come on is a sign of someone interested in a very intense negotiating period before any sexual exchange takes place. An experienced individual initiates an encounter with a partner whom he feels he "can handle"; sexual aggressiveness can dampen as well as heat up a potential encounter.

An example of this dampening process is afforded by a university student who did a "Garfinkelian" study of a bar in Los Angeles.[3] The bar was frequented by "jock type" college males who took a more or less paternalistic approach toward the five-foot, two-inch female doing the study. One strapping male approached her and patted her on the head, saying:

Male: What are you going to be when you grow up?

Female researcher: I'm going to be a damn good fuck.

Male: Ahhhhh . . . I . . . . ahhhhh . . . . [He then turned and walked briskly away. Later he was questioned by another researcher in the study.]

Second researcher: What happened to that short little blond chick you were talking to?

Male: You mean that crazy little bitch? Christ, is she weird; try to talk to her and she comes on like a banshee. Who needs that?

Not only can such aggressiveness have an unnerving effect on a member of the opposite sex (either male or female) but, if done in an uncontrolled manner, will be seen as "crude" and not worth the bother. Generally, the successful initiation is conducted in an enticing manner, but not so aggressively that the individual is seen as either crude or unnerving.

Probably the most common form of initiating an encounter is through body language and eye contact. Specifically, individuals who are not interested in an encounter manifest this through the avoidance of any eye contact, sitting with their possessions (cigarettes, drinks, purse, and so forth) within the immediate confines of their arms or elbows, and in a hunched position (see also Cavan, 1966). This makes it difficult to initiate a conversation or make any kind of contact short of directly approaching them. If they are with friends, the conversation will usually be in lowered tones to avoid being overheard.

On the other hand, individuals who are open to encounters manifest somewhat different body language and conversational activity. Often they will make any eye contact last a little bit longer than normal. Members feel a sort of intensity in this eye contact, or as one individual put it, "She just seems to be staring right into me." Once this sign of availability is given, conversational tones can also increase the possibility of an encounter. If a male has moved to within a few feet of a female, the female may manifest an interest through the intensity of her conversation with her friends. Specifically, a look in the direction of the male accompanied by positive nods of the head or laughter indicates a mutual understanding of the individual's attractiveness. Further, a woman can make a remark loud enough for the male to overhear that indicates her availability. For example, this researcher overheard the following conversation:

Young woman to her female friend: Man, doesn't that music make you want to dance? [Intense eye contact with a man just behind her friend.]

Friend: Yeah, the band is good, but you should have come last Friday night. They had a lead singer that was just great.

Young man: [Introjecting] I just got into town this evening. Is this an example of action around here?

Young woman: Yeah, this is one of the better places. Where are you from?

Young man: Oh, I'm a flight engineer for Southcoast Airlines; I'm just in for a short layover. Got any ideas on how to find some action around here? [Said with a sly, but subtle, smile.]

Young woman: A pilot, huh? I was thinking about being a stewardess. Let's go outside where it's not so noisy and we can talk about this.

Here, body language, eye contact, and the aggressive presentation of a conversational topic by the two women gave a point of entree to the man. In turn, the man gave information about his own background that enabled them to generate a mutually significant topic of conversation, thus facilitating the generation of a viable interaction. In such a manner, subtle social cues are observed and acted upon as signs of an individual's availability—signs of which experienced members are acutely aware.

Given his role of being the more socially aggressive, it is usually incumbent upon the male actually to generate the initial contact with the female. After both members have indicated a mutual availability, a male will often manifest a "building up" behavior prior to approaching a woman. Typically, the male engages in several moments of intense drinking or conversation with friends just before the attempt to initiate an encounter. This behavior is often manifest on a more general level just prior to the band starting to play. After the band has taken a break and numerous males have determined which females they are most interested in, there is a general display of this building-up behavior as the band starts its next set. Males start drinking, talking intensely with friends, and looking in the direction of the female in whom they are interested. Then there is a sort of frenzied attempt to make contact with the female before another male does—a male that is manifesting a similar type of behavior. Such building-up behavior seems to fortify the self-confidence necessary to generate an encounter.

Whether such attempts at generating an encounter are successful, especially at the early stages of the evening, can be crucial to the overall experience of a member. Should the initiation be positively reinforced and his overtures well received, the male may be able to make many encounters during the evening. However, if the first few attempts end in rebuffs and the woman "shoots him down," he tends to have a less positive presentation on the next attempt. A rejection tends to generate a downward cycle of rebuffs and an increasingly negative attitude toward the encounter situation. After a number of such incidents hostility and resentment set in, and the member leaves or goes to a table at the outlying area of the bar to sit out the rest of the evening.

SQUARING OFF AND NEGOTIATIONS

As indicated, the actual interaction must emphasize a presentation of self in which each individual manifests a degree of self-confidence, social competency in fulfilling her or his particular interests, and a level of sexual attractiveness throughout the process. Further, individuals' self-confidence seems to be integrally related to their knowledge of how to fulfill the particular interests of an alter and to align their individual behavior in a manner that best supports their particular interests. As indicated, members frequent bars for numerous reasons: to find an evening of entertainment in drink or dance, to find a brief sexual encounter, and/or to gain a spouse for life. A primary purpose of the negotiation stage is to determine which of these (or what combination of these) interests motivates the alter and how best to make the interests of the alter compatible with the individual's own. All of this must take place in an atmosphere of relatively smooth-flowing interaction with a minimum of faux pas and conversational gaps. Generally, the ultimate interests of the alter are not made explicit until the end of the evening, at the disclosure stage. At that time members indicate an interest in leaving alone, leaving with the individual, or exchanging phone numbers for some future encounter. However, during the negotiations stage each member attempts to gain cues as to the ultimate interest of the alter, although the focus is on maintaining mutual interest and a smooth-flowing interaction.

Along with control of body language and eye contact, members often make use of "side involvements" to generate a smooth-flowing form of interaction (Goffman, 1963: 85-104). By side involvement is meant the casual use of objects such as drinks or cigarettes to fill the gaps in conversations—silences that often make members feel uncomfortable. Invariably members reach for a drink or light their cigarettes when the intensity of the conversation begins to slacken. This shifting from verbal to physical activity gives the impression that action is still taking place and that each member is still interested in maintaining the encounter. This ebb and flow of interaction between verbal and physical actions, if done completely, enables a member to maintain both a smooth-flowing encounter and the interest of the alter.

Probably more important than either body language or the use of side involvements is the generation of conversational topics that are of interest to the other. This is particularly crucial at the initial stages of the encounter because members lack information about alters that can act as a foundation for trust and intimacy. Rather, encounters are built through a successive exchange of information—information that enables members to view alters as more significant and unique. However, at the initial stages of the interaction perception of alters is based on the most cursory modes of information (dress, mannerisms, and so on), and it is difficult to determine a conversational topic that is both relevant and stimulating.

The crucial task of the initial conversation is to generate a statement that is both relevant and requires some sort of a response from the other. In terms of the latter requirement, the use of a question is most common. The old line "Haven't I seen you somewhere before?" is significant because it demonstrates the need for the alter to respond. More importantly, it leaves the alter open to give some indication of an area of personal relevancy. Such a response might include "No, I am from out-of-town and have just moved into the area." Hence, the relevancy of a conversation may now focus on one's past area of residence, reasons for moving, and places of interest in the immediate area.

The problem of generating an appropriate topic of conversation is approached in a number of ways. Three of the more common ways involve: (1) surreptitiously overhearing a conversation and then dropping in a line during a pause, (2) looking for some aspect of alter's presentation that might give a clue as to biographical background, personal interests, and the like, and (3) the generation of conversation based on some aspect of the immediate environment. The overhearing of a conversation between two individuals (e.g., two women sitting at a table) and then interjecting a comment have a number of advantages. Specifically, it enables an individual to gain significant background information prior to an attempt to initiate an encounter. Further, such background information may not only act as a basis for generating a conversation, but also may give cues to the fundamental interest or orientation of the alter. This author witnessed a man overhear a conversation between two women in which one made it quite plain that she has had a fight with her boyfriend and was interested in "really letting loose tonight." In response to this, the man slid into the seat next to her and whispered something in her ear which brought laughter. They were seen leaving together a half hour later.

A second mode of determining a relevant area of conversation is the scrutinizing of the alter's presentation for cues as to biographical background, occupation, and/or personal interests. If the bar is near a university campus, books carried by a student can indicate a course being taken, one's major area of study, and/or personal interests in a particular area. In a similar manner, "working women" tend to dress better and wear more make-up than students, and experienced barroom participants are able to pick them out. Conversations can then be generated relating to their type of work and their personal ambitions for the future. Finally, a wedding ring is often a significant focus for conversation. In a bar within the Western coastal areas, wives of Navy personnel who are at sea will frequent a number of bars for "a little excitement while hubby is away." One bargoer specialized in hustling these "weekend widows"; he would invariably start a conversation with "What would hubby say if he saw you here like this?" The response would often be along the lines of "Well, what he doesn't know won't hurt him."

Finally, if no physical or presentational cues are available, members will often attempt to generate a conversation in terms of the immediate environment (the band, types of people frequenting the place, or "What is that you're drinking?"). These topics are seen to be a sort of last resort, are not particularly interesting, and will often die if they do not lead to something more substantial.

Whatever approach is used, the conversation must be balanced between commonly held topics (e.g., immediate environment) that are usually banal and not of lasting interest, and more esoteric or personal topics that have more potential for interest. Initially, the topic will usually be so general as to ensure some sort of response from the alter. However, if the conversation is to continue and mutual interest be maintained, something of the members' unique interests must be acknowledged. The conversation will usually become structured around some of the more unique interests or experiences of the members, and through the exchange of such information a more intimate and interesting level of interaction can be generated.

A member of the study overheard the following conversation between two young women seated at a table with an interested young man immediately behind one of the women.

Woman [talking to friend while seated at a table]: God, all that he does is work on his new van. He says we'll be able to travel around when he gets it fixed up on the inside, but what am I supposed to do until then?

Woman's friend: Yeah, men have this thing about machines. Sometimes you'd think we're just one more ornament to be polished up and shown off as they drive around.

First woman: Yeah, well, who needs him? I'm just going to have a good time tonight.

Male [overhearing the conversation]: Yeah, some guys just don't know a good thing when they've got it. You just can't ignore someone and expect them to hang around. My girlfriend—ex girlfriend—was a student at the university and all she did was study, no partying at all, what a bore. That didn't last long. You got to have some action. [Pause] This place is kind of slow. I know where there is a party down in the beach area. They have a band and a free keg. We can ride over on my bike, and my friend can take your friend in his car.

First woman [glancing at her friend for confirmation]: Okay, we can always come back if it isn't any good.

Here, a combination of these three strategies is used. Through the overhearing of the two women talking, the male was able to get background information indicating their general intentions for the evening. By claiming a similar background, he was able to generate a level of mutual interest. Further, the evaluation of the present barroom environment as being inferior to a possible party elsewhere enabled the members to focus on an agenda for the evening.

If the negotiations continue beyond the more superficial initial encounter and some genuine interest in the alter is established, members will attempt some kind of pairing behavior. In terms of body language, this pairing behavior is manifest on the dance floor during slow dances in which partners will let their hands slip down around the hip areas of the partner. While seated at a table, members tend to hunch toward each other and talk in lowered tones, which tends to exclude outsiders. This tactility and prolonged close proximity within the pairing situation also may become signs of territorial property. If members decide to leave the partner to go to the restroom, women will often ask the man to hold their purse, cigarettes, or watch their drink. Obviously, the pairing bond is better established when the purse or important articles are left than when just a drink or cigarettes are left behind. In a similar manner, the male will often look directly at any other males in the immediate area in an intense manner, indicating possession of the female. If he goes to the bar to refill the drinks, he will often mention that he will "be right back" in a manner loud enough for any interloper to hear.

Coupled with a general attempt to manifest pairing behavior are the negotiations to determine the "ultimate interests" of the alter. The conversation may drift in areas concerning the alter's boyfriend, husband, whether one has to work in the morning, where one lives, and so on. The alter's availability to a sexual encounter that night is often gleaned from such topics of conversation.

DISCLOSURES AND SETTLEMENTS

The final outcome of this market-place game involves the disclosure of members' "ultimate" intentions and the settlement of gains and losses. This usually occurs around 1:00 to 1:30 a.m., and there is often a marked increase in the shifting of partners just after 12:00 in an effort to determine the most available member for a possible sexual consummation. It is at this point that male members will pressure the female for some disclosure of her availability for a sexual encounter in the immediate or distant future. Unlike the previous stages which were premised on innuendo and tenuous commitment, this final stage requires a disclosure of a member's motives.

According to whether the woman is actually committed to another male (husband or boyfriend), is uninterested in the present encounter, or would like to continue the encounter but at a later date, the particular type of disclosure will differ. Specifically, if the first two situations predominate, she can give the individual a look of shock at the suggestion that she go home with him, give him a phony telephone number and hope she never sees him again, or give some form of excuse. For example, a male and female had been dancing together for about an hour when the bartender said that it was 2:00 and everyone had to leave. This forced the couple to make a decision whether they should continue or terminate the interaction.

Male: You're a lot of fun to be with. Has your friend found herself a friend too?

Female: No, I saw her over at the bar a little while ago. I imagine she is waiting for me.

Male: Oh, why don't you tell her that I'm going to drive you home?

Female: No . . . I'd like to, but I have driven her, so I'm sort of responsible for getting her home.

Male: Well, how about if I follow you and after you have dropped her off, we can go somewhere. Does she live very far from here?

Female: Yeah, she lives clear across town. Besides, it's getting kind of late. I'd like to—maybe I'll see you here next week.

Male: No, I don't come here that often. What's your phone number? I'll call you tomorrow.

Female: We have just moved into a new apartment and don't have a phone yet. But I'll probably be here next week. If you're around, we might get together then.

Male: Oh, okay. We'll see you around. Take care.

Here the female was able to fend off the somewhat aggressive attempts by the male to ensure further interaction that evening. The girlfriend was a useful excuse to avoid further interaction that night, and the claim that there was no phone left the male unsure whether he is being put off or whether she really does not have a phone. Finally, the female structured the immediate termination in a way that left interaction open for the weekend, but precludes it for the interim. This enables her to think over the situation with no obligations on her part. If the male shows up the following week, it may indicate a genuine interest on his part.

Other excuses include, "It's been so much fun, but I have to get up early for work in the morning" or "I don't know you too well now, but if we get together some other time I would really enjoy that." This latter approach implies that future sexual encounters are a possibility, but that they will be conducted under the general normative dating system. By requiring that a dating situation be established before more progress is made toward a sexual encounter, the female can require a higher level of commitment in exchange for the possible encounter. Also she may feel she has more control over the situation and can avoid the potential stigma of having the encounter be simply a "one night stand."[4]

From a male perspective, this is a time in which a member will receive the fruit of his labor or will be shot down. Tempers often run high during this period and fights are most likely to break out. This is especially true of working-class bars in which there are often large holes in the walls of the restrooms, especially right around the urinals. These holes are a result of members putting fists or beer glasses through the wall after being shot down. Further, both the barroom bouncers and the friends of frustrated members will often engage in "cooling out the mark" (Goffman, 1967). Cooling out the mark means that a person has been played along and is suddenly and unquestionably placed in a losing position. The containment of the resultant frustration is first incumbent upon friends, and if this fails, it is incumbent on the formal role of the bouncer. Specifically, a member's friends will emphasize that "it doesn't really matter; she was a dog anyway" or that "there are a lot more around, we can get some more later." If this does not work and the individual is still visibly frustrated and potentially violent, the bouncer will make his presence known and stare down the hostile male. If this does not work, of course, physical force will be used to remove him.

Although violence is a potential aspect of this final stage, the most predominant behavior between males is a verbal recounting of the evening's events to determine whether or not members have had a "good time." This reflecting often takes the form of comparing the number of times a member has asked females to dance or engage in conversation as compared to the number of times he has been positively rewarded for this. However, this sort of accounting orientation is more dominant with novices. The more experienced male members will often reflect on those females that were the more interesting and attempt to generate knowledge as to how to increase the possibilities of an encounter in the future. Discussion with friends will often be in the form of how the particular female struck them, did they have any information on her that might be useful in the future, and any general comments on how to improve a member's chances in that endeavor.

SUMMARY AND CONCLUSIONS

This paper has attempted to outline some of the essential features of the barroom situation, the stages of interaction, and some of the typical tactics taken by members to increase the possibility of an encounter. The barroom situation has been seen to emphasize a maximum of freedom for members to initiate, maintain, and possibly consummate an encounter. Specialized areas afford more experienced members a diverse format for gathering information and generating potential encounters. These specialized areas, e.g., the dance floor, are used by females and males in different ways. Males use the dance floor not only for initiating an encounter (asking a female to dance), but also for gaining information and making contact with other possible encounters. Females, on the other hand, use it for a display of availability or an enticement to other males who are watching them.

Secondly, the market-place encounter has been shown to progress through three basic stages: the initiation, the squaring off and negotiations, and the resolution and settlement. These stages are analytical representations rather than empirical or absolute sequences of events. The episodic and tenuous nature of most barroom interactions precludes the passing of the majority of initiated encounters through all of these stages. Rather, some of the specific tactics used by males and females have been outlined and the importance of theoretical knowledge has been emphasized.

Finally, underlying this paper is the notion that the more experienced members have become conscious of those social competencies that make up the typical orientation that predominates in the market-place bar. In varying degrees experienced members are able to articulate specific tactics and insights that have helped them to fulfill their particular goals. On the whole, most members feel that this knowledge and the freedom afforded members within the barroom situation are only two of the three crucial aspects necessary for successfully consummating a sexual encounter. A third, and very important variable, it is felt, is simple chance or luck in finding a person with similar goals among the multitude that engage in this kind of activity.

NOTES

1. Cavan (1966: throughout) describes three major types of bars: the "territorial bar" (local pub), the "night spot," and the "market-place bar." The territorial bar is characterized as an informal meeting place for individuals, often from the immediate neighborhood. In this setting members can relax, have a few beers, and make casual conversation. Unlike the casual and unstructured environment of the territorial bar, the night spot is characterized as a formal or semi-formal place in which a prearranged program of entertainment is offered and individuals usually bring a partner. Hence, the likelihood of individuals frequenting such places for the express purpose of "hustling" or "scoring" a sexual encounter is rare. The market-place bar is oriented toward singles who are interested in making contact for (at least potentially) sexual encounters.

2. What passes for a marketable aspect of the personality tends to differ somewhat between socioeconomic levels and different subcultures within these levels. Generally, my experience has been with working-class minority, working-class "hippy," and middle-class, white-collar individuals in their twenties and early thirties.

In the case of minorities (blacks and chicanos) there is an emphasis on one's ability to dance, dress sharply, and come on "cool." Given the usual economic position of many minorities in their twenties, ostentatious displays of money are rare, but a general emphasis on style is held in high esteem.

Working-class hippy bars, on the other hand, emphasize a casual informality, a kind of earthy sensuousness, and interpersonal directness. Again, there is little acknowledgment of monetary displays, and sexual overtures are fairly common. Also, the females in these bars are usually more direct and aggressive in their interests in various males for potential sexual encounters.

Middle-class or white-collar bars are frequented by young professionals and the more straight college students. Often young secretaries will be looking for some husband that might be upwardly mobile. Here displays of monetary status are more common with members buying mixed drinks instead of just beer or wine, and males gain prestige by giving waitresses large tips.

Although these various types of bars emphasize different presentations by their members, the purpose of this paper is to analyze the common aspects of most market-place bars. Hence, these aspects are seen as variations of the major structural features outlined in this paper.

3. Garfinkelian study is the determination of commonly held social expectations through the conscious violation of these expectations by a member of the interactional situation. Specifically, Garfinkel has had students "pretend they were boarders at their own homes," "take a drink from another person's cup during a meal," and "require a person to explain themselves during the otherwise most common-sense level of conversation" (Garfinkel, 1967). In each of these cases students have reported a bewilderment and often hostility on the part of the alter, a reaction Garfinkel attributed to the destruction of commonly held and taken-for-granted understandings. In the case mentioned in this paper, the female was breaking a commonly held understanding that females are supposed to be more passive in barroom situations.

4. The problems with stigmatization and the one-night stand are often more of a psychological than a sociological phenomenon. Specifically, members differ as to whether having sexual relations the first night is a sign of immorality. Generally, members seem to feel that this orientation is more predominant in younger females and members from a strong religious and/or rural background. Further, they feel that the invention of birth control devices has decreased the practical problems surrounding sex and has made such "puritanical" perspectives unnecessary.

REFERENCES

CAVAN, S. (1966) Liquor License. Chicago: Aldine.

DOUGLAS, J. (1970) Understanding Everyday Life. Chicago: Aldine.

GARFINKEL, H. (1967) Studies in Ethnomethodology. Englewood Cliffs, N.J.: Prentice-Hall.

GOFFMAN, E. (1967) Interaction Ritual. Garden City, N.Y.: Doubleday.

——— (1963) Behavior in Public Places. New York: Free Press.

——— (1959) The Presentation of Self in Everyday Life. Garden City, N.Y.: Doubleday.

GOLD, R. (1958) "Roles in sociological field observation." Social Forces 36 (March): 217-223.

LYMAN, S. and M. SCOTT (1970) Sociology of the Absurd. New York: Appleton-Century-Crofts.

ORTEGA Y GASSET, J. (1957) The Revolt of the Masses. New York: W. W. Norton.

RIEMER, M. (1949) "The averted gaze." Psychiatric Q. 23: 108-115.

ROEBUCK, J. and S. SPRAY (1967) "The cocktail lounge: a study of heterosexual relations in a public organization." Amer. J. of Sociology (January).

SCHUTZ, A. (1970) On Phenomenology and Social Relations. Chicago: Univ. of Chicago Press.

SIMMEL, G. (1950) The Sociology of Georg Simmel. New York: Free Press.

WEBB, E. (1970) "Unconventionality, triangulation, and inference," in N. K. Denzin (ed.) Sociological Methods: A Source Book. Chicago: Aldine.

BARBARA PONSE is Assistant Professor of Sociology at Washington University. Her research interests include the sociology of deviance, the sociology of sexual behavior, and social gerontology. Dr. Ponse has published several articles on various aspects of lesbian identity, and her doctoral dissertation is an analytic description of identities in the secretive and political activist lesbian worlds.

SECRECY IN THE LESBIAN WORLD

BARBARA PONSE

THIS STUDY is an ethnographic description of secrecy, its accomplishment and effects, among several groups of lesbians. Simmel (1950: 345-346) defines two types of secret societies. The first includes societies whose very existence is not known; the second, pertinent to the lesbian world, refers to groups whose existence is known but whose members are not.

The secrecy surrounding gay life in our society is rooted in the stigma which characterizes homosexual acts and persons. In the following pages I will detail the ways in which secrecy is an inextricable part of lesbian life. This analysis of secrecy among lesbians will concern the ways in which secrecy touches the lives of individual gay women, and the ways that secrecy informs their relationships with both gay and nongay audiences.

The data in this study derive from three years of participant observation in a gay organization, at meetings, parties, in other social settings, and in friendship networks in both activist and secret lesbian communities. Participant observation was supplemented by 75 in-depth interviews with women living in these communities.

Respondents for the interviews were located in one of two ways: either through participant observation in a gay organization or through entry into friendship cliques. The earlier part of the research centered upon women involved with the gay activist group, largely because these women were more accessible than women not so involved. It became clear, however, that gay movement women or "activists" are not representative of lesbians who are not in the movement, particularly with respect to straightforwardness about homosexuality in front of many audiences. Access to nonmovement or "community" lesbians was achieved initially through personal friends who introduced me to their friends and acquaintances; these women in turn referred me to others. Secret community women comprise by far the larger of the two groups in the lesbian world.

The majority of women with whom I talked and whose lives I observed were middle and upper-middle-class, well-educated, and articulate. Participants in the gay organization tended to be somewhat younger than community women; the former also had a heavier concentration of students preparing for a career. The nonactivist community lesbians were mostly professional, holding positions of authority in the business world, academia, and in the arts and professions.

SECRECY, STIGMA, AND AUDIENCES TO THE SELF

In his descriptions of secrecy and secret societies, Simmel (1950: 361, 362) notes characteristic conditions for the development of these societies—conditions which are relevant for understanding the lesbian community. First, a secret society tends to arise under conditions of public "unfreedom" when legal or normative proscriptions regarding persons or behavior necessitate the protectiveness of secrecy. Homosexual activity is proscribed by law, and negatively sanctioned by social custom; homosexual persons are potentially or actually stigmatized in most nonhomosexual settings. Second, a secret society only develops within a society already complete in itself. Lesbian groups exist within the context of the larger heterosexual society, in some ways mirroring its patterns and in some ways opposing them. Third, Simmel (1950: 339) observes that secrecy tends to extend in importance beyond the secret itself and every feature of the secret world. Thus secrecy affects both the internal relations of the people in the gay community and the relations between the participants in gay groups and the members of the larger heterosexual society. This paper focuses on the latter aspect of secrecy.

The perceived need for secrecy stems both from the ever-present possibility of stigmatization and from the perception, prevalent in the lesbian community, or heterosexual hostility toward homosexuality. For the lesbian who wishes to conceal her gay identity; knowing whether an audience is straight or gay is of critical importance. In fact, the relevance of categorizing audiences in terms of sexual orientation is frequently a concomitant of becoming gay. Intrinsic to a sense of gay identity is the definition of oneself as different from heterosexual others, and the realization that one will be defined by straight audiences as different. This sense of difference is accompanied by the realization that disclosure of the gay self is problematic before certain groups. As the secret has profound effects on the social relations of secret keepers, so the definition of an audience as straight or gay has implications both for whether a secretive lesbian will initiate a relationship with a particular audience and for the course such a relationship will subsequently take.

Coming Out

In the argot of the gay community, the initial process of indicating to the self that one is gay is called "coming out." In addition to indicating gayness to the self, coming out refers to disclosing the gay self before an expanding series of audiences. This second usage is more characteristically used by activists, for whom disclosure is part of a political and ideological stance. Secret lesbians as well as activists refer to coming out before various audiences: for example, "I came out with my parents," or "She came out with her straight friends at work."

All lesbians, at the time they come out, are already enmeshed in a network of social relationships with heterosexuals. With respect to these established relationships as well as with new relationships, the issue is whether to conceal or to reveal the newly emergent gay identity. Thus, implicit in the idea of coming out is the progressive disclosure to the gay self, first to the self as its own audience, and then the extension of this disclosure to other trusted audiences.

But disclosure is only one of the responses to secrecy. More commonly, lesbians seek to maintain secrecy by employing strategies such as passing, counterfeit secrecy, restriction, or separation. These strategies are used differently with different audiences to the self; the family of origin, persons known in the world of work, friends and associates, and fellow gays. This paper focuses on each strategy as well as on disclosure and the varying contexts of use.

In and Out of the Closet

In the parlance of the lesbian community, "in the closet" generally means being secretive about the gay self with nongays, although sometimes a lesbian may be in the closet with selected gay audiences as well. One is "all the way in the closet" when only the self is an audience to the gay self or when only the two parties to a gay relationship are aware of the existence of the gay self. One can also be "almost out of the closet" when most significant others know about the gay self. A 56-year-old respondent characterized the closet and her life style related to it:

> There are all kinds of degrees of being in the closet. There are some people who are so in the closet that only they and their lovers know. All the rest of the world is dealing with a masquerade. And then, there are the kind of people I have known, the kind of life I have lived, where you have a circle of gay people that you move around with. And so, you have some social life with them and then there is the rest of the world that you deal with during the week, during the daylight hours.

PASSING: THE MAINTENANCE OF SECRECY

Passing means the successful accomplishment in social interaction of a usual, unremarkable social identity by an individual who would, if discovered, be deemed unusual or different in some crucial way. Passing is being accepted as being "just like everybody else" when in fact some aspect of the person's character or biography if known would serve to set the individual apart from others. Goffman (1963: 2) distinguishes between *virtual* social identity and *actual* social identity. Virtual social identity refers to the self that audiences expect to see. It is self-imputed by an audience, gleaned from perceptible cues generated by an actor. Actual social identity refers to the "real" self that the individual could be demonstrated to be were all the evidence available (Goffman, 1963: 2).[1] In this analysis virtual identity refers to the straight "mask" presented to some audiences by the gay actor while actual identity refers to the gay self.

For the secretive lesbian, passing refers to the accomplishment of a virtual straight identity among straight persons. Passing may entail a variety of strategies on the part of the lesbian, including attentiveness to the details of speech, affect, dress, and demeanor, and, sometimes, the construction of a straight front in concert with male accomplices. On the other hand, such elaborate strategies may be unnecessary since lesbians' secrecy is in part protected by the heterosexual assumption.

The Heterosexual Assumption

A feature of social interaction with straight audiences that facilitates passing is the "heterosexual assumption." The heterosexual assumption means simply that parties to any interaction in straight settings are presumed to be heterosexual unless demonstrated to be otherwise. The pervasiveness of this assumption, in addition to other prevailing norms of social interaction which include, minimally, an agreement to accept interactants at face value, makes it highly improbable that sexual orientation will be raised as in issue. The heterosexual assumption is obviously functional for covert lesbians, though some activist gay women see it as a de facto denial of alternatives in sexuality and life style. Thus a routine assumption of social interaction in the straight world facilitates secrecy for gays in straight settings.

Strategies of Passing

In addition to relying on the efficacy of the heterosexual assumption to obscure the gay self in straight settings, many lesbians employ one or more passing strategies. These strategies may involve impression management, the camouflaging use of dress and demeanor, and sometimes, the conspiracy of others. Often passing requires a conscious management of self, others, and situations. Lyman and Scott (1970: 78) note that passers must develop a heightened awareness of ordinary events and everyday encounters. The covert lesbian who wishes to pass must be concerned not only with obscuring the gay self, but also with presenting a convincing straight front to straight audiences. The woman who wishes to pass must be alive to the subtleties and nuances of communication and relationships. She must be attentive to the details of speech and to other cues to identity in social interaction. The following comment from a 58-year-old woman who has defined herself as lesbian since adolescence, and who, in most straight situations presents a straight image, suggests the extensiveness of impression management involved in passing as well as the tension it can occasion:

> When a person is in the closet they, you know, they're . . . operating on all
> levels, and uh with ah . . . considerable tension. I mean you always know

thirty seconds ahead of what you say, you know what you are going to say. And you get, I got so used to that, I became almost inarticulate when I had a chance to say whatever I wanted to say. I lost a lot of spontaneity of speech because . . . , because I'd formed the habit of always knowing what I was going to say. Changing genders where necessary.

Conversations that are relatively matter-of-fact for straight people may be occasions of elaborate impression management for the secretive gay woman. One strategy used by gays who wish to pass as straight is to remain neutral in the face of detrimental remarks about gay people. Respondents stated that they felt they had silently to withstand casual slanders about gay people or risk drawing attention to their gay selves. Lesbians that I spoke with reported that they often experienced derogatory remarks about gays as being directed, although unwittingly, against themselves.

Simon and Gagnon have noted (1967: 28) that it is easier for gay women to pass than it is for gay men, both because it occasions little suspicion in the straight community for women to live together, and because a category of the "asexual" single woman is both believable and acceptable in the larger society. Some gay women, however, choose to reinforce their straight image by referring to "boyfriends" and/or by having a male friend accompany them on appropriate occasions. The men who serve as legitimating "cover" for gay women are frequently gay themselves. A 52-year-old lesbian recounted the way in which a male friend was used to provide a covering rationale for the lesbian's distress at the time when her 25-year relationship between her and her female lover ended:

> I always took one of the gay fellows to office parties. One in particular, a good friend of mine, is the Vice President of a big company; so we played this game for years and making like he and I had been living together, and during the time the break-up with B——— was going on, my boss threw a big going-away party for one of the guys' 50th birthday and I took along this other gay fellow. And this just threw everyone into a tizzy, you know, and I said well, Tom and I have been having problems, so they would think that all this emotional crisis that I had was over him. It turned out well, they think I had been living with him and all that and they think that's the problem. But it was a terrible thing to have to sit there and you couldn't talk—there was nobody to tell it to.

It is clear from the above that use of a male companion as a cover is functional for maintaining secrecy but, ironically, this very success in passing can exacerbate the subjective sense of isolation. Thus we can see that techniques for maintaining secrecy are a double-edged sword. Secrecy maintenance avoids the problems of stigma and discreditability. Yet passing obviates the possibility of truly intimate interaction with straight people.

Modes of dressing and management of appearance are nonverbal ways of giving information about the self. Thus an important aspect of passing is to conform scrupulously in dress and appearance to the feminine styles prevalent in the straight community. It is not unusual to hear very feminine-appearing lesbians express concern about features of dress which they fear might be clues to the gay self.[2] Dress style and appearance can be used as "protective coloration" to conceal or reveal information about the self.

One respondent spoke about the way in which she would use dress and appearance cues when she felt that her gayness was in danger of being exposed:

> Sometimes I would feel that things were getting a little too close for comfort. I would feel uneasy and uh so I would do the super feminine bit. It's not too difficult for me to do. If I really work myself up to it, I used to be able to do it and enjoy it, but I've had times when I've gotten kind of nervous so I sent up smoke screens as much as possible. You recostume a little bit, you change your mannerisms, you psych yourself out and you bring up topics that are terribly okay, just do the whole thing. It's like guys who are straight but worry about what people think of them and get super-jock. You just select the parts of the role that are the best signals and you send them off (laughter).

Secrecy, Passing, and Member Recognition

The secrecy which is characteristic of lesbian life has implications for gay women's ability to recognize and meet other lesbians. The veils of anonymity are often as effective with one's own as with those from whom one wishes to hide. Thus, an unintended consequence of secrecy is that it isolates members from one another.

It has been emphasized that gay women who are passing must be particularly alert to their audiences. Thus it can be inferred that a gay woman would be more likely than others to spot someone who, like herself, is passing for straight, as she would be aware of the nuances of passing.

People who pass are alive to the cues given off by others who are passing. Among these cues is the recognition of others' passing techniques and strategies. The failure to say certain things—for example, to specify the gender of an individual referred to in a conversation—to be secretive about one's personal life, to express a lack of interest in males, to never having been married, to have a roommate, and to fail to present a male companion at appropriate times can start the speculative ball rolling on the part of a gay woman that another woman may, indeed, herself be gay.

> When I meet new people I generally assume that they are straight. Then if I find out that they are single, have never been married, or have a roommate, I start to wonder . . .

A standard feature of gay lore is that "it takes one to know one." It seems that this is not attributable to any mystical sixth sense but rather to a sensitivity-honed by the experience of passing—to the subtleties of various cues. The following account exemplifies the belief that one can "always tell" one's own, and at the same time indicates some of the pragmatic ways in which gay people go about discerning secretive gays around them.

> I was very closeted and wearing dresses to work and all that and this girl came to work and she really came after me! And I thought it was obvious to everyone in the place. "I'll take you to lunch. Come to my house, we'll have a drink after work," and "tell me about yourself," and it was much more than just your friendship type of thing and when finally I acquiesced, and figured "what the hell," and went over and we had a talk and I asked her, just that, I said, "Well how did you know I possibly would be interested in you?" and she said, "It takes one to know one," and I find that that's true. I usually always . . . in our crowd we used to call it getting a hum, you know, I can always tell if a girl is gay or if she's looking to be turned out [to have a gay affair].

> Perhaps I pick up on this because I'm not bad looking and if a woman is attracted to women, she will look at me in a way that is different or in a way that is different from your heterosexual woman, I guarantee you!

Although the above account is illustrative of the way in which small cues such as eye-signals are put together to identify another gay person, it is highly atypical in suggesting immediate pursuit on the basis of such a hunch. There is, after all, considerable risk that one could be wrong, and gay lore is replete with stories of such mistaken identity. It is usually the instance that such a hunch or intuition about an individual would be followed up by a subtle process of testing the "gay hypothesis" without taking risks to the self or risking disclosure for the other. Some women refer to this inferential process as "dropping pins," by which is meant the casual mention of gay places, gay people, or gay events. If the person responds by acknowledging ("picking up the pin")—that she knows the persons, places, or events—it is tentatively assumed that she is gay. This inferential process usually takes place with seeming nonchalance and in an indirect manner, so that at any point up to the actual verbal disclosure of the gay self, parties to an interaction can signal that they are "really" not gay after all and withdraw with impunity. As may be imagined, these negotiations frequently take place with straight audiences being none the wiser. The process for establishing interactants as secretly gay is such that alternative explanations can be proffered up to the point of denouement. There is no overt admission or talk of gayness, and the usual indirect approach presents little threat to the secretive status of either party.[3] It is true, however, that many secretive gay women feel that it is too dangerous to engage in such identification games in straight settings; and in such instances secrecy is effective in concealing the gay self no only from the straight world, but also from other gays as well.

The World of Work

The necessity for passing may be perceived as more or less urgent with respect to particular audiences of friends and acquaintances. The consequences for the breach of secrecy are seen as more grave in some circumstances than in others. The world of work is a setting where most lesbians feel constrained to pass as straight. Typically the work world is a straight environment in which the lesbian must keep her gay self hidden.[4] The consequences of disclosing the gay self to work audiences may reach far beyond disapprobation to include the curtailment of a whole career; thus, the necessity of maintaining secrecy about the gay self places considerable strain on what might appear to be extremely ordinary situations involving coworkers. For example, conversations about relationships or leisure-time activities can be problematic for the secretive lesbian. Casual exchanges about social life can constrain the gay woman to being noncommittal about her friendships and associations.

The perceived need for secrecy about a gay identity in work settings can have profound effects on establishing extrawork relationships with colleagues. This problem becomes exacerbated when the successful negotiation of one's business career involves business-connected sociability, increasingly a feature of many professional and business circles as the individual's career advances. One woman, prominent in the field of public relations, when asked how she handled business-connected entertaining, answered:

> I haven't handled it very well up until now. I haven't done any business entertaining at home and that's a subject that's about to come up, because

> we've just moved and taken an apartment where I now can entertain quite easily . . . and I'm not quite sure, how I can handle it—It's quite a problem on my mind right now. . . . Most of the people with whom I'm associated in business are *very* conservative in every respect. . . . I know specifically that my boss in particular has a big thing against gay women, because he's been very overt about it, never dreaming that he's stepping on any toes. I've been very uncomfortable. I never give in to the urge to say anything and I don't like that: there is a great deal of discomfort for me in any kind of dishonesty.

Some professions are regarded as more "sensitive" with respect to gayness than others. Women in the teaching profession, for example, and women who work with children feel particularly constrained to be very secretive about their lesbianism in the work world. Several women whose work is involved in some capacity with a school district stated that they feel inhibited about becoming involved actively or noticeably in the gay community: they fear that, if they become identified as gay, they might be fired. The following respondent indicated that although she was with the activists "in spirit," she herself could not be an activist for these reasons:

> (I am) aligned with the gay movement in the terms that the feminist movement is. But as far as being active—no. At the present time my reasons would be self-protectiveness, in terms of, I don't know if it's a cop-out or not, but in terms of my employment, and . . . I work for (a large public organization) and I work in the school system in the area, and I think there would be negative repercussions if I were active and found to be active, by my agency, and yeah, I'm not willing to take the risk. I could not be an open activist in the Gay Movement, I cannot be on the barricades there at the present time, um, and in some respects I doubt that I would be at any time in the near future.

The need for wearing a straight mask in the world of work is part of the gay folklore—a folklore which is documented by the experiences of some gay women. Among the lesbians I interviewed, two had been expelled from college and one had lost a teaching position for reasons related to lesbianism. But even among women who have not had such a personal experience, the experiences of others, the stories which circulate about such incidents, and a pervasive belief in the likelihood of negative consequences accompanying disclosure in the work world are strong deterrents against revealing the gay self to this particular audience. In turn, this prohibition against revealing the gay self in work situations serves to prevent the work world from being a source of sociable relationships.

Counterfeit Secrecy

Lesbians who conceal their gayness from straight audiences usually express the conviction that the attempt at secrecy is effective and that the straight masks they present are unquestionably accepted. However, in the experience of some of these women, relationships with friends and family are more accurately characterized as patterned by the tacit negotiation of mutual pretense through which the gay self is not acknowledged. I call this pretense "counterfeit secrecy."

Glaser and Strauss (1965: 64-78), in their discussion of awareness contexts, refer to the state of silent "collusion" between actor and audience as a "mutual pretense awareness context," whereby both parties to an interaction know a secret but maintain the fiction that they do not know it. Both audience and gay actor cooperate to maintain a particular definition of the situation and both parties tacitly agree not to make what is implicit, explicit by direct reference to it.

Emerson (1970) notes the function of such tacit negotiations in smoothing over a potentially disruptive breach of social expectations. She remarks that social actors frequently prefer to ignore a violation of social expectations and to act as if "nothing unusual is happening" in order to maintain the flow of interaction. Emerson's observations illuminate an important aspect of social interaction which gives rise to counterfeit secrecy. Straight audiences often act as if "nothing unusual is happening" when presented with gay people or gay situations, providing that no one makes the implicit, explicit. Making the violation obvious, by naming it or pointing it out, would of course force acknowledgment of the pretense.

A respondent in her late fifties commented on the quality of counterfeit secrecy in her relationships with straight friends and neighbors:

Were you open about being gay? Well you know, certainly not verbally, no. But it was that life that so many of us had led. Technically "in the closet" but where the neighbors, the people you work with, have to know! How can they avoid—but they don't want to put it into words: "Don't tell me, don't tell me." But they would ask my friend what she was going to cook for dinner, and I would interchange with neighborhood men about how to fix the lawnmower, how to build this and that (laughter) and we're talking. . . . It was role playing that we had not constructed but they simply sensed that these were the appropriate people to talk to these things about. We used to be just aghast at the assumptions that these people acted on, and yet uh nothing was ever said . . . it seems that people are willing to take you as you are if you just don't burden them with any names.[5]

Thus if lesbianism was not explicitly referred to, interaction flowed smoothly, suggesting a kind of acceptance. However, this seeming knowledge and seeming acceptance cannot be tested for fear of rejection: the whole structure of this ambiguous acceptance is founded upon not acknowledging the gay self, and thereby functions to confound the very possibility of disclosure. In this way, the etiquette of counterfeit secrecy entails a posture of discretion which becomes more and more difficult to disrupt as time passes.

Although counterfeit secrecy undoubtedly facilitates the appearance of amicable relations, knowing that one is excluded from confidence has impact upon the behavior of those who interact with gay people. The person who has not been granted the right to know is also constrained not to admit knowing that which has never been acknowledged. The relationship between the concealer and the person from whom something is concealed is weakened by the facsimile of secrecy. A barrier, paralleling the barrier of real secrecy, is thereby raised against real intimacy by counterfeit secrecy.

THE FAMILY OF ORIGIN

After a woman has come out and acknowledged herself a lesbian, she is confronted with decisions as to which audiences she should reveal her gay identity. Few audiences rival the place of the family in terms of intimacy and importance to the individual. The typical intimacy of family relations creates its own pressures toward disclosure. Simmel (1950: 335) notes that intimacy in relations makes secret keeping difficult and contains many impulses to disclose. Thus, the family of origin is of particular salience to the lesbian with respect to secrecy and disclosure. Disclosure of the gay self to the family of origin, however, raises the specter of rejection from an audience that a lesbian may consider important. The lesbian typically (and often not incorrectly) has an image of her family as disapproving heterosexuals.

The family, both in terms of proximity and intimacy, is so situated that the management of secrecy is difficult, and the gay self may be inadvertently revealed. During the time a young woman is living at home there are many more opportunities for the family to observe her and to draw conclusions about her personal life and relationships than would be the case if she lived away from home. Occasionally, discovery of the gay identity by the family may occur dramatically, as it did for one young woman whose spurned lover called her parents:[6]

I had been seeing this woman for about a year, and the relationship ended on a rather sour note. She called my parents and informed them that I was a lesbian. It was terrible. I didn't know what to do at the time. They thought maybe I should go to California and that it would help me to get over this relationship, this woman. They always thought it was other people that were exerting a bad influence on me. They thought that going away would keep me away from those influences.

The consequences of ruptured secrecy, or inadvertent disclosure of the gay self, may be that future references to the gay self and acknowledgment of the lesbian's personal life are proscribed within the family. The gay self is considered "off bounds" as a legitimate topic of conversation; the lesbian is unacknowledged as a lesbian by her family. Thus, counterfeit secrecy commonly limits relationships between the lesbian and her family.

For the gay woman, counterfeit secrecy entails many of the same consequences for interaction with others as does actual secrecy. If, in order to maintain a relationship, one must obscure or deny the "true self," the implication is clear that the true self is unacceptable. Such relationships, no matter how intimate in terms of conventional social roles, are thus limited in their intimacy. Lesbians who maintain counterfeit secrecy with their families affirm that they feel cut off from being themselves, just as do gay women who maintain real secrecy. The context of counterfeit secrecy, especially the fear of disapproval, renders the family unavailable to provide emotional support to the lesbian and thus serves to attentuate relationships in ways quite similar to real secrecy.

DENIAL

An important comcomitant of counterfeit secrecy is denial on the part of the family or others. Denial may be manifested by continued questioning of the gay woman about boyfriends, by references to future marriage, or by other tactics which presume the heterosexuality of the lesbian. Denial is instanced in the following account by a lesbian whose mother had been apprised of her daughter's lesbianism:

My mother will ask me occasionally, "how is your love life dear? Have you met any nice boys?" And I can just see her clapping her hands over her ears and saying inside, "Oh please! Don't tell me!" And I don't. I just say, "Oh it's fine," or "Yeah, groovy!" It's an unspoken thing in our house. We don't talk about things like that. *My brother used to know, but we never talk about it. There are boundaries on the things we talk about. It's funny how people know and refuse to know, and won't talk about it.*

In the experiences of some lesbians, parents and family think of the lesbian as "sick" and hope for a "cure."

> My parents sent me to a psychiatrist to be cured. He said, "I don't know what your parents want me to cure you from." To this day, that's the way they think about it, as something to be cured from. "You can't be happy. There is no way you can be a lesbian and be happy," they think. That's all they pray for, a big miracle. I mean that's the way they perceive it. But I tell her, "Mother," I said, "What is happiness for you is not happiness for me." We don't talk about it . . . it used to really bother me but it's gotten to the point where she's more unhappy than I could ever be. . . . There is nothing I can do about it. I have done my best to try and get her to accept it, you know. I've said to her, "You've got a good kid. She's doing good things and she's bright and she's got a nice home and I've got nice friends and I'm telling you I'm happy." But it's not enough . . . I can't change her. I finally came to terms with the fact that it was her trip, not mine.

In sum, for many lesbians, relations with family members are strained because of the family's perceived lack of acknowledgment or acceptance of lesbianism. Secrecy, counterfeit secrecy, and the tensions generated by the acknowledgment of an unacceptable gay identity may all result in the lesbian feeling separated or cut off from her relatives. As the above accounts illustrate, the modal pattern of relationships between the lesbian and her family of origin was counterfeit secrecy combined with an implicit denial of the woman's homosexuality.[7]

Handling Secrecy: Restriction and Separation

Besides passing, other ways of handling secrecy with respect to particular (straight) audiences (and occasionally, "untrustworthy" gays) can be typified as follows: restriction—straight persons may be restricted as audiences to the gay self, that is, they are categorically inadmissible as personal friends; separation—audiences may be kept separate from one another, where gay friends are segregated from straights with the latter usually unaware of the existence of the former.

RESTRICTION

Among the women with whom I spoke, a few preferred to avoid straight people altogether as potential friends. For these women, the world of work provided the single avenue of contact with straight people, and these relationships were maintained at an instrumental level only.

Extrawork relationships with coworkers were discouraged. In a very special sense, the real lives of these secretive lesbians are spent with gay people in gay spaces. (See Warren, 1974, for an extensive description of gay time and gay space.) The times, places, and people that are significant to these women are all gay. In line with Simmel's observations about the intensity of relations among secret sharers, the gay audiences before whom the straight mask is dropped assume great importance for the hidden lesbian (Simmel, 1950: 360). Correspondingly, gay time and gay space are given a greater accent of reality. It is only before gay persons in gay places that the authentic self is revealed. Lesbians whose world of sociability is exclusively gay describe themselves as living a "totally gay life."

Not surprisingly, women who segregate themselves from contacts with the straight world perceive the greatest differences between the categories gay and straight, and express the greatest social distance from the straight world. Simmel (1950: 365) and Warren (1974: 6, 141) both note that secrecy may promote the sense of superiority in the way of life of the secret group. This was exemplified in the comment of one gay woman who maintained she had nothing in common with straight people:

> When I'm around straight people, I can be very shy and uncomfortable, because I can't be myself. So it's probably all tied together. I like gay people more, to me they're much more interesting, maybe because I'm able to talk about myself and my marriage so that makes them more interesting.[8]

SEPARATION

Most of the lesbians in both secretive and activist communities did not want to isolate themselves from friendships with straight people. Yet initiating or maintaining relationships with heterosexuals confronts the lesbian with decisions about disclosure or concealment of her gay identity. Both lines of action entail tension. Disclosure risks the possibility of rejection, and concealment carries the tension of secrecy and conscious management of the self. Many of the lesbians with whom I spoke elected to handle these tensions by keeping their gay lives and straight friends separate, revealing the gay self only to gay audiences and donning a heterosexual mask for straight friends.

Within the community, the segregation of gay and straight friendship worlds is described by lesbians as "living a double life":

> Oh boy, I've lived a double life like you wouldn't believe all my life and sometimes the pressure was so enormous I thought I was going to explode.

> We'd sit around and have coffee, the girls in the office, and they'd say . . . this woman looks like a man . . . Omygod that's a queer and I'd sit there and listen to this kind of stuff and . . . until I'd just get violent sometimes. And there's been a few times when it's been all I could do just to keep from jumping up and saying, "Look you guys have lunch with me, we've socialized together for fifteen years. I'm queer!" I've wanted to do it so bad that you know, I uh, almost explode! Because you know . . . Why? I mean, what would I have accomplished anyway—I would have lost more than I had gained.

The above respondent expressed with a great deal of feeling the twin themes of the frustration imposed by secrecy and the certitude of rejection by straight friends should the gay self be revealed that is typical of community women.

Among activist women, though not to the extent characteristic of community women, leading a double life did occur. Being secretive among one's friends and at the same time an activist in the gay community was experienced as dissonant by these women. One activist lesbian, unwilling to reveal her gay self to straight friends, expressed the incongruity between her political and personal life when acting as a group leader at an activist meeting:

> This is hard for me. I am the leader (of the discussion group) and I wish I were in a better place as an example. I feel very gay, I live an entirely gay life style, that is my involvement sexually as well as socially is with women, with a woman. And yet I am not entirely comfortable with my gayness. For example, my neighbor is like a sister to me, I've known her for ten years and yet I have never told her I am gay. I am very closed about being gay with many people. It has gotten better over the years. I go back twenty years being gay. I don't feel entirely comfortable within myself about it . . . in terms of sharing it and yet more and more of my life is devoted to making it possible for gays to live without oppression.

The separation of gay and straight worlds is the typical pattern among community lesbians and is characteristic of some activist women as well. Although this tactic engenders a subjective dissonance and the conflict of "disloyalty" to activist gay audiences (if not to straight audiences as well), it allows the maintenance of relationships inside both heterosexual and homosexual groups with minimal risk of rejection from either.

Living a double life can be accompanied by a sense of alienation—and can escalate the fear of discovery. Not only must the secretive lesbian be an audience to the deprecation of gay people (which she may interpret as "really" directed at her) but she must also be able skillfully to negotiate relationships so that straight friends remain unaware of gay friends. Thus a double life requires the most stringent management not only of the self, but of situations and others who might give clues to the gay self. Relationships with the straight world, though uninterrupted, are nonetheless thinner when the "true self" must be concealed. At the same time, though gay friends are privy to the gay self, their friendship claims may be limited by the extent to which the gay actor is committed to maintaining friendships in the straight world; for, under the conditions of living a double life, sociable time must be divided between gay and straight friends, and straight friends must be handled in such a way that they are unaware of the existence of the individual's commitment to the gay world. This boundary between gay and straight friendship worlds comes to be zealously guarded, not always to the advantage of gay friends, as the following account illustrates:

> At a party one evening a group of women discussed the disadvantages of people dropping in without notice.
>
> Sometimes, if I'm not expecting anyone I won't answer the door. I think it's terrible, what if you are entertaining some straight friends or something and some big dyke comes in. You know, people tell me I shouldn't feel that way, that I'm ashamed, of my friends, and well, maybe I am, I don't know, I just feel that way." Another woman concurred: "no, no! I can understand it, I mean. You have to choose who you're going to tell, you have to keep things separate, I mean I agree with you."

Many gay women experience the fearfulness of disclosing the gay self to straight friends as alienating. Obviously, secrecy precludes the possibility of social supports from the straight world. A community lesbian spoke about the lack of acknowledgment and social supports in terms of opression:

> Well, like most oppressed people I didn't realize it. Now I realize that my private life wasn't okay. To have to sit around and go to endless wedding and baby showers and buy gifts and things and no one celebrated my emotional highs with me . . . and uh then when you are in an emotional hole, there is no one to hold your hand as any woman can expect when she breaks up with her boyfriend.

Such lack of reciprocal sharing in straight/gay relationships tends to promote a sense of isolation; and the gay woman may see herself successively cut off from meaningful interaction with heterosexual others while correspondingly strengthening her bonds with the community of lesbians.

DISCLOSURE

Passing, restriction, and separation all involve the keeping of the secret. Disclosure, on the other hand, involves revealing the secret to given audiences. The most salient distinction that gay women make with respect to audiences to the self is to categorize them as either straight (heterosexual, i.e., potentially hostile) or gay (homosexual, i.e., potentially friendly). This distinction is particularly important with respect to making friends and building friendship networks, as the intimacy of friendship relations escalates the tension toward disclosing a gay identity. Goffman (1963: 20-31) distinguishes between the "own" and the "wise" as two categories of ingroup and outgroup persons (Goffman's general term for nondeviant outgroup individuals is "normals"). The own are the ingroup, whose members share both the stigma and the secrecy of stigma. The wise are those outgroup persons who know ingroup secrets—they have been effective in piercing secrecy. Within the lesbian community, even more subtle discriminations are made: not all of one's own are considered trusted audiences to the gay self, and would therefore, like straight (i.e., normal) audiences, be presented with a straight mask.

Four of the women with whom I spoke have never revealed their gayness to straight friends even in relationships of considerable duration. Considerably more of my respondents, however, expressed great apprehension about having their gayness revealed to *further* audiences of straight people although they had straight friends who were aware of their gayness. Subsequent disclosures do not necessarily become easier despite having experienced acceptance from heterosexual friends previously.

The timing of disclosure is considered problematic by many. To disclose the gay self at the beginning of a relationship with nongays runs the risk of immediate rejection by a relatively "untested" audience, and opens up the possibility of accusations of being "blatant." To wait until a relationship has been established, on the other hand, means that the secretly gay woman may be accused of dishonesty in her relationships with her friends. Thus lesbians who wish to maintain or initiate relationships with the straight world perceive themselves in a "damned if I do, damned if I don't" situation.

The social meanings of disclosing the gay self to straight audiences can only be adequately appreciated with reference to the secrecy of which it is an opposite. Disclosure of the gay self occurs with an awareness that the secret once revealed cannot be hidden again. Disclosure also means that with every person to whom the secret is revealed, a trust is given in which the risk of further disclosure is inherent. Nonetheless some lesbians do select particular straight audiences to whom they reveal the gay self.

Some audiences of heterosexuals are differentiated by members of the lesbian community as being safer than others for the presentation of a gay self. These include straight people with whom the relationship predates coming out; straight friends who have successfully demonstrated the qualities of empathy and discretion; feminists who are ideologically encouraged (or constrained) not to stigmatize lesbians and to be supportive of the lesbian life style. Special audiences of straight persons such as therapists or lawyers are usually considered safe audiences to the gay self.

One activist lesbian remarked that the pressure within certain feminist groups toward acceptance of lesbianism as an alternative life style helped mitigate, for her, the risks of disclosure:

> You know if I've gotten bad reactions (from disclosure) I don't know about it. But you have to remember that I'm doing this mostly with feminists and there would be a certain kind of social pressure on them from other people if they indicated that it did bother them. They're in a funny position right now because they supposedly can't think that there's anything the matter with (lesbianism).

Disclosure to straight friends is usually a gradual process. Some lesbians report some preliminary "feeling out" of their audience prior to disclosing. An audience to whom a gay identity is to be revealed might be sounded about their attitudes toward gay people or toward minorities in general. A "stage setting" tactic reported by several respondents was to engage a prospective audience in conversation about prejudices against "minority groups." Agreement about the "unfairness" of prejudice would create the background for the revelation of the gay self.

Modes of Disclosure

Modes of disclosure include both direct and indirect verbal and nonverbal forms. For example, the family's awareness of the gay self usually occurs through observation of cues rather than by direct disclosure on the part of the lesbian. As already indicated, the family as a close audience to the gay self is ideally situated to notice cues to the gay self.

A respondent after years of secrecy described the method of disclosure by implication that she had initiated with straight friends.

> If it is quite clear up front that this is part of my life, then I don't have to go through all that crap with these people, little stupid games of easing into it, getting to know someone really well and then trying to figure out you know like how do I break it to them, because I may lose this friendship, because it'll be too much for them or I can ignore it and never state it and always have a huge chunk of other things I'm stifling. . . . I don't come out and say "I'm a lesbian." But when I'd come in with someone it would be pretty clear. I'd say "she and I have done this," or "she and I had done that," I'd try and be as natural as I would be with a guy, if I was going with a guy, but not having to make this, blowing trumpets, making an announcement when I walk into the room.

The above account illustrates that implication and inference may be the vehicle by which the gay self is disclosed. Such a technique entails simply no longer hiding the gay self. The straight audience is presented with the everyday concerns accompanying the gay self or with cues to the woman's gay identity.

ROLE PLAYING AS NONVERBAL DISCLOSURE

One of the most important ways of negotiating an image is by the manipulation of appearance and dress. Affecting a masculine appearance is an aspect of role playing, as this term is used in the lesbian community. "Butch" and "femme" refer, respectively, to masculine and feminine roles in the lesbian community. Although the terms have reference primarily to a division of labor and constellations of behaviors based on heterosexual models, they may include styles of dress and mannerisms. The butch woman affects a masculine style of dress and mannerisms; the femme, a stereotypically feminine mode of dress and comportment. The butch mode of dressing has characteristically served a minority of gay women as a nonverbal means of announcing gay identity to others. The adaptation of the butch role, insofar as that includes distinctive clothing styles, reveals the gay self to other lesbians and often to heterosexuals as well. The presentation of an identifiably gay style has repercussions in the lesbian world as well as in the straight world. It may serve to circumscribe relations with more secretive lesbians. Since it is likely that gayness could be imputed on the basis of association alone, a very secretive lesbian would avoid being seen with any obviously gay friends. Such women state that they are fearful that associations with identifiably gay persons may evoke suspicions about their own gayness.

One woman, in referring to friends that she described as very butchy looking, stated:

> Now they don't go—they don't have anything to do with straight people, and truly sometimes I was embarassed to be with them. They were so butchy looking—I felt like I didn't want to go out with them to the store—What if we should meet some straight friends or something? I'm ashamed to admit it—It's shitty to feel that way about friends but I can't help it.

Although the tactics of concealing one's friendships with other gay people was widely accepted as expedient, understandable, and even necessary for the preservation of secrecy, it was nonetheless an intense experience for many gay women.

It is clear, therefore, that the perceived necessity for secrecy influences the selection of friends in the gay world as well as in the straight world. Highly secretive lesbians cannot afford to have extensive relationships with men and women who are obviously gay. In addition to meeting other criteria for friendship, gay friends must be chosen with an eye to the convincingness of their straight masks and to their lack of detectability in the straight world.

VERBAL DISCLOSURE

A critical feature in most accounts of disclosure is the emphasis placed on the *verbal assertion of gayness*. It is "putting it into words" that marks the irrevocable breaking of secrecy. According to this logic, behaviors and situations are capable of multiple interpretations and imputations, but words are not. Frequently, it is only through such a verbal assertion that a straight audience will be acknowledged by a gay actor as "really knowing" and it is through words that counterfeit secrecy may be forfeited or broken. Knowing the gay self through direct disclosure by the gay actor is distinguished by many gay women from all forms of proximate knowledge such as strong suspicions, guessing, or hunches. Thus disclosure to straight friends—precisely because of the importance and irrevocability it entails— may serve to intensify the bonds of friendship. The friend becomes the wise and shares the special knowledge of a secret world. The intensity which marks the relations of secret keepers is thereby extended to special audiences not intrinsically part of the secret world.

Disclosure as an Ideology

Disclosure has a special emphasis in the lesbian community at the present time, and both secretive and activist lesbians have developed lines of action in response to this special emphasis. The tension between secrecy and disclosure among lesbians exemplifies Simmel's (1950: 333) observation that disclosure is always just under the surface of secrecy, creating a constant tension toward breaking the secret. Simmel (1950) asserts that pressures develop in secret societies that predispose their members toward disclosure: as these societies sustain themselves, enduring over time, the strength of assertion comes to replace the protection of secrecy.

Over the past several years, with the advent of both gay liberation and the rise of the feminist movement, there has been increasing resentment against the structures of secrecy. An ethos of openness has been developing in certain parts of the gay community. This phenomenon has evoked a wide range of responses from within the community. The reactions of the secretive lesbian community toward activists and activism span the range of possibilities (with the exception of disinterest). One woman in her sixties, who remains quite secretive about her own gayness with straight friends and family, nevertheless expressed enthusiasm for what she perceived as a movement toward legitimation of homosexuality through the new openness about gayness by activists:

> You asked me how I felt about the gay liberation thing and I'll tell you I think you have to go overboard on anything, way overboard, before you go to the extreme—before you back up, then you're a step ahead of where you were before and this is why I have such a faith in the kids—nothing is going to change till we go to these extremes. . . . You have to demonstrate, you have to make a scene before you make the slightest impression on anybody.

Lesbians such as the one quoted above categorically state that secrecy is the worst feature of gay life. Paradoxically, some women who find secrecy oppressive also find the openness in the gay activist community to be very threatening. They feel that activism will draw attention to gay women who heretofore went largely unnoticed.

> Most of the time they associated homosexuality with men and now you know they've started looking at women and—before we were kind of back over here and it never occurred that two women—two women who aren't even gay at all probably have people looking at them and I'd just as soon not have that kind of attention. What's the benefit of it? Because nobody is really going to accept this. Not in my lifetime.

Other lesbians state that they cannot identify with the activists either on the basis of activist techniques or personal style. Some emphasize what they perceive as class differences between themselves and the activists, and characterize activist lesbians as "having nothing to lose."

> And you see the public is still not seeing that there are good and bad in this life, too. And unfortunately the ones they've seen aren't ones I'd run around with either, at least some of the ones I've seen on television, why they're not my caliber that I would associate with. . . . . You get a lot of mouthy women up there, who go hollering around and they're obnoxious—some of—a lot of them are—I guess they are out there fighting the battle for us but I'd rather see some women up there who look like women, presidents of companies that had responsible jobs saying their piece on a little higher plane.

Many secretive lesbians—like the one quoted above—have an ambivalent attitude toward secrecy, perceiving its necessity and at the same time desiring disclosure from the "right" kind of people to educate the public about the diverse individuals under the umbrella of homosexuality.

Lesbians whose secret status depends upon the ignorance about lesbianism in the heterosexual world fear the liberationists who emphasize the "truth about gayness." For their part activist lesbians develop rationales to account for their openness, which they express in political terms. In a political sense—they maintain—disclosure is a "consciousness-raising technique" making people aware of gayness as a life style, while at the same time it is a refusal to hide the gay self. According to some gay activists, concealing the gay self is tantamount to being ashamed of it.

Most overt activists say that they feel a sense of personal freedom in no longer having to mask their gay identity.[9] However, they do acknowledge that "doors may be closed to them" in the future for having done so. On the other hand, most activists observe that identifying people by sexual orientation is in itself oppressive and thus consider this emphasis on disclosure a temporary, situated phenomenon which at some future point will no longer be necessary.

> I feel that it was necessary to state that I was a lesbian because it's almost like flaunting it and why would I flaunt that sort of thing, and um I'm hoping that I'll reach a point in say three years where I won't ever have to designate myself by any stupid arbitrary word . . . but politically, it's absolutely essential, because every time I say that (I'm a lesbian) it's so much easier for someone . . . who doesn't feel free . . . to be whoever they are, someone who spends all their time hiding. It makes it so much easier for them to be comfortable with it, comfortable with themselves.

SUMMARY AND CONCLUSIONS

The lesbian creates her social identity in a matrix of secrecy and disclosure. She may choose to conceal her gay self by passing, or by restriction and separation of the audiences to the self. The emergence of the gay self thus renders the presentation of the self problematic. The lesbian must take into account the factors of stigma and the risks attendant to the revelation of her gay identity in most social settings apart from the community of her own.

It has been emphasized throughout this paper that one of the most significant aspects of being or becoming gay is that it alters fundamentally the relationship of the self to others, based upon the perception of hostility toward gayness on the part of heterosexual society. The relationship of the gay self to the straight world is mediated through secrecy. Secrecy in turn further isolates the gay self from straight others and binds it closely to its own.

The requisites of secrecy necessitate the categorization of others as gay or straight. These become the primary typifications through which interaction is filtered. The interactive process of indicating to the self that the self is gay, that the other is gay or straight, serves to reiterate the primacy of these categories. Concomitantly, the process of bringing into awareness the gay self serves continuously to elaborate its importance.

Warren observed that the stigmatization of the gay world ensures that all gay space and time will tend toward secrecy (Warren, 1974: 18). This paper demonstrates the multiple ways through which secrecy intensifies commitment to the gay self and binds the gay self to the gay world.

By the same token, the importance of disclosure and assertion newly emphasized in sectors of the gay community is grounded in the context of the secrecy of that world. Simmel (1950) emphasizes that the allure of disclosure inheres in secrecy. Thus secrecy itself impels toward its own destruction. But in addition to secrecy containing the seeds of revelation, factors that develop within the secret society militate toward disclosure. The posture of the secret society toward the larger society is ultimately one of vulnerability: the possibility of discovery threatens the safety it offers. Thus, Simmel (1950) asserts that if a society is to survive, the strength of assertion must take the place of secrecy.

The initial phases of the new ethos of openness continue to reverberate throughout the gay community. With it, new definitions of gay identity are emerging. Although there is hardly a rush out of the closets, it is likely that the process of disclosure on an individual level and on the community level will continue. The process of disclosure will, in turn, continue to demystify and depolarize what still remains a hidden and secret world.

NOTES

1. Note that Goffman's definition of the real self is that which corresponds to prevalent social categories, a difference in perspective from the existential sociologist who locates the real self in the actor's meanings of self.

2. Not surprisingly, lesbians express relief about the current relaxation of dress codes within the straight community, which make casualness if not ambiguity in women's clothing the norm. Thus dress styles have, within limits, become a much less precise indicator of the gay self than formerly.

3. Lyman and Scott (1970: 80) call this process the giving of signs of a double identity. These signs should be such that they can be withdrawn or redefined should "pure passing" become necessary.

4. The rise of gay liberation and gay advocate organizations has led to the advent of the "professional gay," an individual whose professional status derives from the status of being gay—i.e., as an editor of a gay publication. The professional gay is distinguished from the gay professional—an individual who, in addition to being an incumbent of a professional occupational role, happens to be a gay person.

5. "Friend" in this context is partner in a gay "marriage."

6. Lover: the term used among lesbians to designate parties to a sexually and socially intimate relationship.

7. Similar disclosure and secrecy problems obtain with the family of procreation of the women I interviewed who had children of their own from a previous (heterosexual) marriage, or who had been involved with another woman who had children.

8. Marriage: a monogamous relationship with another woman in this case.

9. However, the activist lesbian tends to express an empathetic understanding of more secretive lesbians. More likely than not, the activist herself has audiences with whom she is in the closet.

REFERENCES

DANK, B. (1971) "Coming out in the gay world." Psychiatry 34 (May): 180ff.
EMERSON, J. P. (1970) "Nothing unusual is happening," pp. 208-222 in T. Shibutani (ed.) Human Nature and Collective Behavior, papers in honor of Herbert Blumer. Englewood Cliffs, N.J.: Prentice-Hall.

GAGNON, J. M. and W. SIMON (1968) "Homosexuality: the formulation of sociological perspectives," pp. 349-361 in M. Lefton, J. K. Skipper, Jr., and C. H. McGaghy (eds.) Approaches to Deviance: Theories, Concepts and Research Findings. New York: Appleton-Century-Crofts.

GLASER, B. G. and A. L. STRAUSS (1965) Awareness of Dying. Chicago: Aldine.

GOFFMAN, E. (1963) Stigma, Notes on the Management of Spoiled Identity. Englewood Cliffs, N.J.: Prentice-Hall.

——— (1959) The Presentation of Self in Everyday Life. New York: Anchor Books.

LYMAN, S. M. and M. SCOTT (1970) A Sociology of the Absurd. New York: Appleton-Century-Crofts.

SCHUTZ, A. (1973) Collected Papers I: The Problem of Social Reality. The Hague: Martinus Nijhoff.

SIMMEL, G. (1950) The Sociology of Georg Simmel (K. H. Wolff, ed. and trans.). New York: Free Press.

SIMON, W. and J. H. GAGNON (1967) "Femininity in the lesbian community." Social Problems 14, 2 (Fall): 212-221.

WARREN, C.A.B. (1974) Identity and Community in the Gay World. New York: Wiley-Intersciences.

PHILIP W. BLUMSTEIN is Associate Professor of Sociology and Director of the Center for Studies in Social Psychology at the University of Washington. His research interests include the analysis of microsocial processes and the study of the social context of human sexuality.

PEPPER SCHWARTZ is Assistant Professor of Sociology at the University of Washington. She is currently beginning a comparative study of homosexual and heterosexual couples (with P. W. Blumstein), continuing her interests in the family, sex roles, and human sexuality.

BISEXUALITY IN MEN

PHILIP W. BLUMSTEIN
PEPPER SCHWARTZ

CURRENT SANCTIONS against homosexual behavior in men reflect a broad pattern of stigma attached to any deviation from the male sex-role. Popular understanding of the concept "masculinity" implies that one must show erotic distaste (not merely neutrality) toward other males, and that one must demonstrate competent performance in the heterosexual arena. Just as overt homosexual behavior implies impaired masculinity in the popular imagination, so too, any failure of proper male sex-role enactment suggests an increased likelihood of homosexuality. Androgynous appearance, "effeminate" gestures or mannerisms, a typically female occupation, or any of a number of other gender-inappropriate behaviors are likely to label a man homosexual. Conversely, homosexuals without gender-inappropriate gestures, occupations, or

AUTHORS' NOTE: This paper is intended as a companion piece to the authors' "Bisexuality in Women" (see Blumstein and Schwartz, 1976).

patterns of grooming and attire often successfully pass as heterosexual, if they so choose, as long as they are able to conceal that part of their behavior that is overtly homosexual. It is almost necessary for them to be "caught in the act" (or be associated with some suspect milieu or social group) before a sexual identity imputation is leveled.

Whatever the source of the popular cultural belief that masculinity is a coherent entity across a number of behavioral and emotional dimensions, examples abound which ought to invalidate that notion. However, most thinking about male sexuality is intolerant of ambiguity and fails to recognize that the sexual landscape is inhabited by persons who do not fit into dichotomous categories. For example, there are indeed men who can and do routinely engage in both heterosexual and homosexual behaviors. When such people come to public attention they are called bisexuals. But since the concept of bisexuality fits so badly into simple dichotomous thinking about sexuality, evidence of its existence in a person's biography must be almost inescapable before the term is applied as a label. Otherwise the individual is characterized in some other fashion, e.g., "He is a homosexual unable or unwilling to accept his *true* identity."

This dichotomous thinking has woven its way into our language, and indeed, if we are not careful, misidentifies the phenomenon of people who are attracted to members of both sexes. In common speech, bisexuality often implies that a person's sexual behavior and/or attraction is equally divided between men and women. Our research, however, has shown that most people are less orderly in their sexual behavior, and so we have come to prefer the term ambisexual, implying some degree of erotic responsiveness to members of both genders. Unfortunately, bisexual is the term in common usage, and so we have adopted it for this paper. But it should be understood that it merely means some degree of eroticization of both genders. We should note that the individual may not share this definition, nor call himself bisexual; rather, he may claim to be heterosexual or homosexual, with some ability to sexualize the other gender. Later in this paper we will suggest why one self-label is chosen over another.

Because bisexuality does damage to an otherwise neat and uncomplicated conceptual apparatus, it is not surprising that it has received very little scientific attention. But it is a little more surprising when we consider how much evidence of bisexuality has been unsystematically amassed. According to Kinsey et al. (1948: 650-651), 25% of the male population of the United States had had "more than incidental homosexual experience or reactions for at least three years between the ages of 16 and 55," only 10% were "more or less exclusively homosexual" during the similar time span, and only 4% were exclusively homosexual throughout their lives.[1] These data illustrate three important points: first, a person may have a significant "mix" of heterosexual and homosexual responses in his lifetime; second, there is a good deal more adult homosexual behavior than there is lasting homosexual identification; and third, a period of significant homosexual responsiveness does not necessarily determine one's future sexual orientation, and homosexual behavior must therefore be a less potent life-organizing force than common stereotypes would lead us to believe.[2]

These data were not alone in reflecting the existence of a bisexual phenomenon. Studies of prison life (e.g., Kirkham, 1971; Lindner, 1948; Sykes, 1958) have shown that previously exclusively heterosexual men can have fully developed liaisons of various kinds with other men while institutionalized, but will discontinue all behavior that could be termed homosexual upon release. Yet homosexual prison experience seldom disposes inmates to a homosexual self-identification or even occasional homosexual acts on the outside (Lindner, 1948).

Humphreys' (1970) well-known study of sexual transactions in public restrooms elaborated a different but complementary point concerning the inclusion of erotic variety into the patterns of activity of an individual. A number of Humphreys' "tearoom" participants were married to women and had families, but engaged routinely in anonymous sex in restrooms in parks, and many reported very satisfactory ongoing sexual relations with their wives.[3] Some of Humphreys' sample considered themselves homosexuals involved in a marriage of convenience; others considered themselves bisexual ; while others described themselves as heterosexuals who had found a compromise solution to meet their erotic needs. Nevertheless, there was a large number who routinely engaged in both heterosexual and homosexual behavior.[4]

Humphreys' data, as well as the prison studies, underscore another important theme in male sexuality. Many men have both the ability, and often the preference for engaging in anonymous or "impersonal" sex. While the motivation for seeking such an outlet is complex and poorly understood, nevertheless, the subjective experience reported by many males who engage in tearoom activities is that of a purely physical urge which causes their pursuit of anonymous sex.[5] Although women are socialized to believe that sex should occur within the context of love and commitment, men are seldom sensitized to such constraints. There is a popular image that the male "sex drive" is able to overwhelm the self-control of an individual and therefore dire personal and social consequences follow from failure to achieve sexual release. While sex within the confines of an ongoing relationship may have decided virtues, such opportunity may be unavailable or "more trouble than it is worth," and hence tearooms, prostitution, steambaths, and similar institutions have developed (Weinberg and Williams, 1975). Thus, for example, while homosexuality is seriously tabooed, the unavailability of women in prison, coupled with the ideology of the male sex-drive, contribute to a set of cognitive and interactive patterns that vitiate for many prisoners the sanctions against homosexuality, and free them from having to see the causal locus of their homosexual behavior as reflective of their "true sexuality." Similarly, teen-age hustlers who have homosexual relationships with older men often do not view themselves as homosexual, largely because of the depersonalization of the other and the financial gain that can be understood to have motivated the behavior (Reiss, 1961).

All these scattered studies have pointed to the existence of something called bisexuality, but none has undertaken to investigate the topic in its own right. In an initial attempt to remedy this oversight, we undertook an interview study of bisexual behavior and sexual identity. The remainder of this paper is organized to reflect our most consistent finding concerning both male and female bisexuality: the fact that there seems to the outside observer to be little coherent relationship between the amount and "mix" of homosexual and heterosexual behavior in a person's biography and that person's choice to label himself or herself as bisexual, homosexual, or heterosexual. We will try to address the question of why certain sexual patterns lead to one form of identification or another, with special attention to the impact of the highly stigmatized quality of male homosexuality in American society.

The observations made in the remainder of this article are based on interviews with 150 persons (equally divided between males and females), who have had more than incidental sexual experience with members of both sexes. Interviews were conducted in Seattle, New York, Berkeley, San Francisco, and a few other locations between 1973 and 1975. The sample ranged in age from 19 to 62, and represented a wide variety of occupations, educational levels, and patterns of sexual experience. Most of the sample were recruited through advertisements in taverns, restaurants, churches, universities, and voluntary associations. A large group of respondents were from a "snowball" sample and from personal contacts of the authors. Interviews lasted between 1 1/2 and 3 hours and were transcribed verbatim and coded. The anonymous interviews dealt with the respondent's sexual behaviors and fantasies, and critical events in the formation of a sexual identity. We also interviewed a large number of persons who were not bisexual but who had strong feelings on the subject of bisexuality. In the remainder of this paper we will present some of the empirical regularities we observed among male respondents, beginning with those who identified themselves as bisexual, and then proceeding to those with homosexual and heterosexual identifications.

SEXUAL BEHAVIOR AMONG
SELF-IDENTIFIED BISEXUAL MEN

The lack of continuity between different aspects of sexuality made it common that male respondents, using the seven-point Kinsey rating system, would give quite different responses when rating their sexual history, their current sexual behavior, their patterns of love, and the sexual label they felt most comfortable applying to themselves. A large number of men in our sample were firmly committed to a bisexual identity even though their recent erotic histories (or in some cases their entire erotic histories) were almost exclusively homosexual or heterosexual. Given the intense stigma attached to homosexuality among men, we were prepared to find that some of our respondents with primarily homosexual experience would call themselves bisexual. Since homosexual is such a negative label, it is not surprising that men with meager heterosexual histories might be tempted to avoid its use.

Predominantly Heterosexual Experience

What was surprising, however, was the substantial number of respondents with bisexual identities, but little or no homosexual experience. For many of these men there was an articulate ideological rationale supporting their identification. Some of these men, harking back to what they had learned in psychology courses, felt that all people were "inherently" bisexual, and their failure to act on this part of their nature simply reflected societal inhibition. They felt they had a potential for homosexual behavior and they were simply waiting for their libidinal liberation to catch up with their sociopolitical ideology, or for the "right man to come along." For example, one man expressed his feelings this way:

> I guess I'd say I'm between a "one" and a "two" [predominantly heterosexual, with some homosexuality, on the Kinsey seven-point rating

scale]. That would be more like my head than my behavior. I mean I have those feelings, but I don't express them much. . . . I sort of ascribe to the notion that there is this male and female in all of us. I don't pick up on it often, probably because of some negative stuff about homosexuality, but I'm sure the potential is there.

Another clearly stated his beliefs about what was "politically correct." He had been in a "men's group" and lived with an ardent feminist woman.

I put myself at number "three" [equally homosexual and heterosexual on the Kinsey scale]. To me, it has meant being more sensitive, more open to people . . . another form of communication. It's a non-sexist lifestyle. I've read a lot of Kinsey and worked in sex education and this seems to me like the natural progression. The whole anti-homosexual thing is just social oppression.

Another feminist male respondent reported:

I think bisexual orientation grows, and the gay feelings have been generated initially through head-tripping, and a lot of just political thinking about what was going on, through the women's movement and the spin-off of that.

For some other men, it was not an ideological position, but rather the single or few homosexual experiences themselves that encouraged the adoption of a bisexual identification. Even though an experience might be rare or unique, the fact that homosexual enjoyment had been able to occur informed the person about his true nature. He was forced to reevaluate his sexual preferences. Many of these men at first thought or feared that their single adult experience indicated they would become totally homosexual. But subsequent heterosexual arousal and enjoyment of heterosexual coitus (often part of a test aimed at rejecting the homosexual hypothesis) suggested bisexuality as an appropriate explanation. For example, one respondent noted:

When I went and had sex with Tom I had trouble processing it. I knew I must be gay. . . . But then it didn't happen again and I still kept noticing women on the street and things like that and I still was horny for Sheila. So I looked around for another explanation. I didn't know the word "bisexual" until recently, but that was the feeling I came to about myself.

Another described a summer spent with a male college friend with whom he was having a sexual relationship:

We'd go around and hustle women all day, trying to prove to each other and ourselves, I think, that it was O.K. And we'd make sure we were appealing to women, and get into make-out sessions, and we would really get turned on.

Some men found that it was not simply the continued erotic appeal of women that prevented them from taking on a homosexual identity. Their own conception of what a homosexual was was so far from their self-conception that they had to cast around for another interpretation of their own behavior. For example:

> I was attracted to men at this time, but it didn't worry me. I'm pretty easy-going and I don't worry about things. Besides, I had heard the term "queer," but I didn't identify with it at that time because that meant somebody who was really effeminate, somebody who minced around a lot, somebody who would run home before their parents got home, went into their closet, and put on their mother's dresses. I knew that didn't apply to me.

Predominantly Homosexual Experience

Self-identified bisexual with predominantly homosexual experiences are difficult to discuss because of the negative sanctions and potential demoralizing impact for some males of accepting a homosexual identification. much of heterosexual society, and almost all of homosexual society, is suspicious of a man who participates in homosexual behavior while claiming to be other than exclusively homosexual. For example, when one respondent was asked if people were dubious about his continued heterosexual interest after initial homosexual experiences, he responded:

> Yes. I've got that kind of feeling and feedback from people. . . . Straight people are more or less dubious about bisexuality. You are either one way or the other, and that's it. And in some instances you have more trouble convincing . . . the gay person, the homosexual. [They say] you can't enjoy sexual relationships with men and women. It's harder to convince a gay person than a straight person.

Another respondent noted that heterosexuals were more likely to feel that he was trying to excuse his homosexuality by calling himself bisexual:

> It was really incredible. After I told my parents about Al they asked me if I felt bad about never having children. And I said to them I might have children because I still liked women sexually. And that really upset them because they thought there was hope, and they told me to see a psychiatrist so I might someday be able to have a happy married life. I tried to stress that it wasn't an either/or choice. But they said it just showed how confused I was and that I needed help so I could resolve this problem.

The skepticism with which many claims to being bisexual were met reflects our dichotomous notions of sexuality, as well as the "logic" that homosexual reactions eradicate heterosexual responsiveness, and the idea that heterosexuality is superior to homosexuality (i.e., when given a free option one would always choose to be heterosexual). Therefore, most of our cultural thinking demands significant heterosexual credentials before a homosexual label can be skirted. Much of society is willing to disbelieve an uncredentialed assertion of bisexuality, and attributes such a claim to the inability to come to grips with a homosexual label. For instance, one respondent felt that homosexuals he had met did not believe in bisexuality:

> Gay people are prone to think you're either one way or the other and that's it. I think it's more trouble convincing a gay person that you are bi than convincing a straight person. Gays think you're just trying to escape the "real you," and lots of guys have done this whole spiel on me about "accepting myself," and accept being gay and crap like that.

The cultural suspicion of bisexuality places the researcher in a difficult interpretive position. While it is true that many of the people who identify themselves as bisexual (with little heterosexual experience) are truly attracted to and sexually responsive to both genders, it is also true that a bisexual identity is sometimes a way-station in the process of accepting a homosexual self-identity. In interviewing these two types of respondents, it is indeed almost impossible to determine if a person is in a "stage," a defensive posture, or a permanent bisexual life style. Consequently, we will make no judgment concerning the part homosexual defensiveness plays in bisexual identification, or how "real" bisexuality is for an individual respondent. As we have pointed out, many of the relevant respondents were aware of the doubt and lack of social validation their bisexual identification received. Some said they chose to be unconcerned about others' doubts, while some were very introspective, trying to reconcile what they thought they felt to be true with the interpretations of others.

Ambivalence in the Homosexual Community

It is in the male homosexual community that bisexual males without much validating heterosexual experience suffered the greatest challenge to their identities (Warren, 1974). Among the gay activist elements of the community there is often a political rejection of bisexuality, since failure to assume a homosexual identity is viewed as contrary to gay liberation. Another concern is that bisexuality is dangerous in homosexual relationships because one's bisexual lover might retreat to heterosexuality if the stigma, interpersonal pressures, or psychic pressures become excessive. As one respondent stated:

> Gay men don't trust bisexual men because they see them as basically playing a game. They're seen as not really seriously committed to other men, and so in a context where people's affections are vied for, [they believe] a woman will draw the allegiances of a bisexual man in preference to another man; so a lot of men don't feel very safe; it's not a safe place for emotional work.

In a male homosexual community there is a great readiness to disbelieve and denigrate a person's assertion of being bisexual (Warren, 1974), while at the same time a curiously grudging esteem for credentialed bisexuals. Not surprisingly, subcultural meanings focusing on many aspects of male sexuality have a prominent place in the homosexual community. As in the heterosexual society at large, assumptions that sexuality is dichotomous and that sex-object choice reflects one's masculinity are part of homosexual erotic folklore. Consequently, bisexuality is a conceptual complication that is difficult to assimilate. Since it is common for male homosexuals to think of homosexual responsiveness as mutually exclusive, they tend to ignore any heterosexual interests of their own, and they interpret previous heterosexual behavior as discontinuous with respect to their "true sexuality."[6] Thus, using themselves as an inferential basis for role taking (a kind of projective stereotyping) they fail to find credible the possible coexistence of two kinds of erotic sentiments in others, and are therefore inclined to attribute to the bisexual other dispositions, such as antihomosexual defensiveness or fear of stigma (Warren, 1974). As one homosexual stated:

> I really think that bisexuality is just a defense against being called homosexual. Most of these guys go through a period before they come out for real, and they go back and forth and they think they really like it both ways. But they usually *really* prefer one or the other sex so much more that calling themselves bisexual is just a liberal euphemism or a gay cop-out. I do not think I personally have ever met anyone I would call bisexual.

On the other hand, there is some belief in the rare occurrence of bisexuality; a "real bisexual" is held in begrudging esteem because of the centrality of masculinity and masculine imagery in the gay world. If members do not hold masculinity to be of paramount importance in their own self-evaluation (most members do, and in this respect are reflecting again the continuity in male sexuality between heterosexual and homosexual contexts), they will, for the most part, hold it to be central in those to be esteemed and sought as sex partners. Because of the significance of masculinity, and because heterosexual competence is seen by many homosexuals to be a crucial sign of masculinity, the assertion of bisexuality is viewed as a claim to high erotic worth. At the same time, however, such a claim signals a rejection of the homosexual community and one's commitment to it, and consequently social distance from it (Warren, 1974). Thus, like many other claims to exalted status, it is likely to be met with ridicule and disbelief. Bisexual status is easy to claim, but the claimant must undergird the credibility of his assertion with external evidence. He may wear a wedding ring, discuss a wife (rather than abstractly speaking of his bisexuality), flaunt a particularly masculine occupation, or indicate his independence of the gay world by not appearing in it too frequently. Nevertheless, he is likely to meet with disbelief because he is in effect saying he is "more masculine than thou" to men who cannot compete with him on these criteria. He is not playing by the rules by which masculinity offers a source of erotic worth in the homosexual community, but is reaping the rewards in terms of prestige and sexual opportunities that would not be open to him as a self-defined homosexual. At the same time, he is reflecting his autonomy with respect to the homosexual community and in some sense stating that he is better than it, which causes a back-lash reaction among his peers. For example, one primarily homosexual respondent reacted in the following manner:

> Most of the people that describe themselves as bisexual come off to me as simply trying to make themselves more attractive to other homosexuals because there seems to be some sort of thing about bisexuals being very sexy.... I'm not sure why that is. There seems to be something that goes hand in hand with masculinity and heterosexual orientation.... Hetero-sexuality just seems to naturally occur with masculinity and the two are sort of equated even by people who consciously deny that there is that connection. Unconsciously they do believe it and they are more likely going to be attracted in terms of whatever masculinity is.

Herein, then, lies the tension in the homosexual community concerning bisexual men. Herein also lies the ambivalent feelings of bisexual men toward the gay community. To the extent that their prestige is enhanced there, the community. To the extent that it is a major source of sexual outlets, it is attractive. But to the extent that the bisexual is treated as a creature apart, and is continually being challenged in his claims to bisexual status, it is an alienating environment and one not conducive to the maintenance of a bisexual identification.

These pressures on the bisexual from the homosexual community have several consequences. Persons may choose to flaunt their bisexuality and try to make it believable, they may keep their bisexuality a secret from most members of the homosexual community (and thereby run the risk of its subsequent discovery and possible disruption of developing relationships), or they may avoid the organized homosexual community entirely. Another possible consequence is that the critical stance of the homosexual community inhibits the individual from labeling himself as bisexual and provides a vocabulary for discounting potential heterosexual responsiveness. In this way, membership in the gay community in some cases can encourage a man's rejection of any personal sense of bisexuality.[7] One man expressed it this way:

> When I told Alan I thought I was bi, he told me I'd better get my head on straight and he sent me to the gay counseling center. Richard told me that I shouldn't feel so guilty about being gay and that I would get over the need to want to keep a foot in both worlds. Steve told me to stop trying to pretend I was so butch. I started to think they knew me better than I knew myself, and I didn't go out with another woman until I left New York and that whole group of friends.

Overcoming the Dichotomy

Many homosexuals, like their heterosexual counterparts, believe that for most people "one drop" of homosexuality makes one totally homosexual. In attributional terms, since homosexual behavior is not something one would choose voluntarily (considering the costs involved), its slightest evidence must indicate some deep dispositional feature of the individual. We heard this logic applied both to others and to oneself by a number of bisexuals and homosexuals. This logic, combined with the notion that homosexual interest means heterosexual disinterest, would suggest that a number of fairly powerful contravening factors ought to be in operation among persons who maintain a bisexual identity. Among our respondents whose identification was bisexual and who had a fairly significant amount of both heterosexual and homosexual experience, we observed the following common patterns:

(1) Most had had more than simply sexual experience with both genders. For example, heterosexually married men with years of tearoom experience reported that they adopted a bisexual identity only when they began to interact *more than genitally* with male sex partners. To spend the night, or even a few hours, in the other's home often accompanied the beginning of a move away from an exclusively heterosexual identification. While the relationships these men had with other men might continue to be defined as purely sexual and transitory, nevertheless they were more

than purely genital. The heterosexual experiences of these men were likely to be even more involved. Most of the men had been married or engaged, and all reported having been in love with at least one woman.

(2) A sizable minority of respondents had not been socialized to attach shame or stigma to homosexual behavior. A number of respondents reported early childhood involvements with other males which had no sense of guilt. Homosexuality became stigmatized for them only in late adolescence or early adulthood at a time when their homosexual feelings were fairly well structured. These men also reported that they had active dating patterns and were very much involved with heterosexual courtship. They had never seen courtship as a sham to cover up their homosexuality, since for them homosexual behavior might require discretion, but it did not produce guilt or anxiety. Somehow, these people felt they had escaped the logic that holds that homosexual behavior is a refutation of heterosexual interest. They had to face the choice of their "true sexuality" only at an adult age where the question itself was uncompelling because of the backlog of experience to which it contrasted. As one man put it:

> I had the reputation in high school as being a stud. I don't know if that was accurate but I was having sex with women, which I think was more than most of the other guys. I would also occasionally go to the gay bar, especially when I was broke, and get those guys to buy me a drink, and sometimes I would go home with one of them if they were not too old or fat. I figured "What the hell?" Didn't bother me any.

(3) Some men had had a period of homosexual activity in adolescence coterminous with heavy involvement in heterosexual courtship, followed by an exclusively heterosexual phase, then followed by a new interest in homosexual activity. These men reported that homosexual activity seemed a natural part of adolescence, but as heterosexual courtship became more serious it seemed reasonable to discontinue activity with their peers. For most of them it was not reported guilt that curtailed these activities, but rather a sense of movement into an "adult phase" when one left childish activities behind. Nevertheless they held pleasant recollections of the homosexuality of their adolescence. As one man recalled,

> I was sixteen and I developed a really close friendship with two other guys. We became the "unholy trio." We snuck beer, we went out and got drunk together, we joined a frat together, we went out on dates and tripled, and we did everything together. We used to go drive out together looking for trouble to get into and sometimes two of us would drive up to these caves . . . and roll out our sleeping bags, and set there and bullshit and have a couple of six-packs . . . and it was great, just great. Pretty soon because we slept in the

raw and the closeness of the sleeping bags, and feeling so close, we ended up masturbating each other and even kissing. We always felt good about it although we never talked about it. There was definitely a three musketeers feeling—we were much closer to each other than the girls we dated. I really loved the two of them. . . . But it was definitely an adolescent thing. Once we got to the point where we got seriously into girls, that was *it*.

(4) A fairly infrequent way of embarking upon a bisexual orientation was through group-sex interactions. Although this pattern was very commong among women, it was rare for men. This is not to say that men are absent from, or uninterested in, group sex. Quite the contrary, these events are usually planned and orchestrated by males for the enjoyment of males. The anticipated scenario, however, is for the male to be surrounded by women; while there might be a homosexual motive present on some level, it is certainly seldom on any level that is observable to the participants or to social researchers. In fact, most group-sex settings described to us were assiduously antihomosexual when it came to the males, but prohomosexual when it came to the females. This reflects a number of themes in sexuality, including the threat that male homosexuality has for males in our society, and the relative lack of threat that female homosexuality holds for males and females (Blumstein and Schwartz, 1976).

Nevertheless, some men reported that the generalized erotic tension of group sex, coupled with a permissive and hedonistic ambience, allowed them to learn to enjoy behavior they would never ordinarily have considered. Once enjoyed, some chose to incorporate the experience into a set of sexual self-definitions and labels, while other respondents chose to focus on it as unique and uninformative about their sexuality. This latter group, of course, do not think of themselves as bisexual. Of the former, one man described his experience this way:

> I never realized before there was something special about being able to touch a man. At first I resented Lillian taking my hand and placing it on Bill. But I got into it and felt terribly warm and close to him. . . . I didn't care who was touching what. I felt incredibly in touch with myself and with him. It felt, and I still feel, that it changed me.

Males were more likely to maintain an uninterrupted bisexual self-definition once the label was adopted than were female bisexuals. This probably reflects the women's greater commitment to norms of sexual monogamy. It was not uncommon for women to express the irrelevance of the label "bisexual" except when they were between steady partners: they were bisexual when unattached, but heterosexual when they were involved with a man and homosexual when with a woman. Males, on the other hand, seemed to be keeping their prospects open, even when monogamously involved, and reported being erotically attuned to both men and women even when not in active pursuit. It was common for bisexual men to report moods in which they needed heterosexual contact (if they were in a steady homosexual relationship) or, more commonly, homosexual contact (if they were involved heterosexually). One married man remarked:

> It just depended on my mood. When I'm particularly depressed—which happens only maybe every eight days (and I don't mean profoundly depressed)—but when I catch myself just sort of staring blankly out the window ... then I know that's a time when I need to be with a man. ... I cannot particularly explain it, but that's real.

Of course, the respondents varied in the ease which they allowed themselves to meet these needs. However, they all reported that homosexual needs were much more easily met, given the differences in the two marketplaces.

HETEROSEXUAL BEHAVIOR AMONG
SELF-IDENTIFIED HOMOSEXUAL MEN

Some self-identified homosexual men who engaged in occasional heterosexual relations resemble in most details a comparable set of self-identified bisexuals. Many such men expressed a political reason for the choice of the homosexual identification, arguing that the gay movement needs its adherents to present an undiluted public image. They also noted that it is because of their homosexual behavior and feelings that they are stigmatized and for which they are seeking liberation. Therefore, they feel it is necessary to identify themselves by their minority group status. For example, the head of a men's group put it this way:

> If I tell people I'm living with a woman they'll say, "Well no wonder he's not effeminate," or "No wonder he's so up-front about gay rights. He's just a liberal; he's not a queer." I didn't want a cop-out for me or for them. I tell people I'm a faggot because it's what they need to hear. I want to be on the front lines on this thing and bisexuality is begging the issue.

Many homosexual men who have heterosexual relations choose to keep their homosexual identity because of what they see as significant differences in their two kinds of sexual responses. Most of those we spoke to were not heterosexually active as adolescents and their first heterosexual encounters occurred after they had been actively homosexual for a number of years and felt they were completely comfortable with their homosexuality. In almost all cases, their female partners were personal friends prior to the eroticization of the relationship and knew fully about the respondent's homosexuality. For example, one homosexual respondent stated:

> This woman and I would get high together and have a good time. She was bisexual and we both knew where our heads were at. But one night it just seemed like the thing to do. I was curious and I knew it would not be a big hassle about love, the future, et cetera, with her. It was a good experience.

Many of these respondents expressed the feeling that it was only once they were comfortable with their homosexuality that they were able to engage in heterosexual relations. In coming to grips with their homosexuality, they felt they had come to grips, as well, with their own sense of masculinity and were not concerned with the implications of the judgments of the heterosexual world for their masculine self-conception. One man stated:

> When I joined the Air Force and being in a totally masculine environment I started to relate to men more spontaneously and feel better about my own masculinity. I felt I bridged a gap between me and the straight males—not sexually, but like being one of the guys and trusting each other. And as a result, all sorts of blocks broke down. I seemed to start to notice women. Why, I don't know. For the first time in my life I started having sex dreams with women in them. I was still mostly turned on by men, but suddenly, women too. It surprised the hell out of me.

For these men the prospect of possible failure in a heterosexual encounter was not anxiety provoking. This was partly due to their self-definition as homosexual; the heterosexual encounter was an irrelevancy, and therefore failure or success did not matter. Their confidence in their ability to perform adequately in their own sexual arena was what mattered to them. Thus, no amount of heterosexual failure would undermine their own sense of erotic competence. For these men, like so many who were actively involved in the organized homosexual community, their sense of competence as a sexual performer was a core feature of their self-identity. They also expressed the feeling that because the possibility of failure with a women was not anxiety provoking, then failure was less likely to occur, and therefore they could enjoy the experience. There was a great deal of variation in the degree of enjoyment and the extent to which the behavior became regularized. One man said:

> I never realized how soft a woman's body is. I found the whole thing a different but good sensation. We did it pretty often. I had worried about keeping an erection, but it was no problem. . . . It was just a friendship, so there was no pressure.

Another respondent gave a somewhat different impression:

> I enjoyed it [sex with a woman friend] because I liked her, but it was not nearly as exciting as with a man. I missed the kind of athletic thing with a man and some other things that are obvious. It was hard to keep my attention from wandering. It was OK, but just not that satisfying.

Most of these men felt their heterosexual behavior did not really make them bisexual because of the emotional context and meaning of the sexual relations. These men did not place their female partners into the "trick" category (i.e., a person one chooses for purely sexual purposes, with no necessary implication of a repeated sexual encounter or a developing social relationship). This was partly because the female was already at least a close acquaintance, and partly because the high level of sexual arousal found with "tricking" was absent with the female friend. Nor did these men place the women in the category of persons with whom they would like to escalate a sexual encounter into a courtship or an affair. The sexual tension found in the early stages of homosexual courtship was not present, and the men felt that other men were the only persons with whom they could form a lasting relationship. The women were most likely to be placed into the category usually reserved for homosexual male friends with whom one might occasionally engage in comfortable but not highly erotically tense sexual relations. As one respondent expressed it, "an old friend you might just fall in bed with. Something might happen, or you just might go to sleep." Just as the male peers in this category were neither highly eroticized nor romanticized, the same was true of the women in the category. They were a diversion, but not a core feature in the respondents' sex life.

HOMOSEXUAL BEHAVIOR AMONG SELF-IDENTIFIED HETEROSEXUAL MEN

Much of this type of behavior has been described by other researchers as noted above (e.g., Humphreys, 1970; Lindner, 1948; Reiss, 1961;

Troiden, 1974). For the most part, few of our respondents fell into this category, especially since persons of this type are least likely to take part in a study such as ours. What we did encounter were men who would admit to homosexual activities in certain circumscribed circumstances but who still felt they were completely heterosexual. Some of these were men who were able to respond to other men in the context of group sex, but because males never entered their sexual fantasies, because there were drugs or alcohol involved in the group-sex setting, or because the respondent would never pursue a homosexual encounter or be attracted to a man in any other context, these respondents were able to see themselves as exclusively heterosexual.[8] For the most part, such men did not seem to be defensive on the subject of homosexuality in general, and seemed perfectly willing to discuss with us their homosexual experiences. So the claim that they were simply unwilling to admit to homosexuality does not seem totally reasonable. For example, one man described his life in this fashion:

> I love my wife. But I think I like sex a lot more than her, and anyhow I'm on the road a lot. It's easy just to get some sex along the way and it's easier with men. I never spend the night . . . I never kiss them. It's just sex, and they do all the work.

A fairly large number of the men who claimed a bisexual or homosexual identity recalled periods when they engaged in homosexual activities but used rationalizations to avoid having to face a homosexual identification. Some of these limited their activities to tearooms, others had been male prostitutes, and still others went to gay bars or steambaths, but only when very drunk. Many of them performed only the insertor role (i.e., the "male role"), and often limited their behavior to being the insertor in acts of fellatio where they had no nongenital bodily involvement. In all of these cases, elaborate vocabularies of rationalization were evolved to insulate the heterosexual identity from assault, for example, "I would have preferred a woman if it weren't so much harder to make out," or "Only the guy who *gets* screwed is queer," or "I wouldn't need men if my wife would give me the kinds of sex I like," and so on. All of these respondents had changed identities to bisexual or homosexual before we interviewed them, and the great majority had modified their homosexual behavior to include a wider variety of sexual acts and a greater potential for emotional involvement with partners. Since we spoke to very few respondents with similar histories but who did not move toward a bisexual identification, we are unable to suggest what factors differentiated these two patterns. The very fact that a large number of bisexual respondents would have claimed to be heterosexual (even though their behavior was far from exclusively so) if we had interviewed them at an earlier point in their lives, illustrates, again, the malleability and temporal unpredictability of sexuality and sexual identity.

CONCLUSION

We have offered a summary of some of the regularities we observed among our respondents. From these regularities several factors are suggested that ought to be part of any theory of bisexuality to be developed. The first of these is the meaning and significance of masculinity in American society. Certainly we need a richer understanding of masculinity before we can say anything more definitive about male sexuality. We need to know about the external events and internal processes, both psychological and physiological, that enter into an individual male's sense of his own masculinity. What are the cultural and subcultural understandings that allow him to make sense out of the information his body is giving him? How do such processes of sense making affect his behavior in the erotic and nonerotic spheres? How do cultural understandings of sexual arousal and erotic behavior diverge from scientific understandings?

Another essential part of any theory of bisexuality is a treatment of the effects of sexual stigma, stigma avoidance, and being defined as "different" among the already stigmatized. It is important to focus on processes of labeling and self-labeling and how they interact with social constructions of bisexuality and sexual motivation. A third essential part of any theory of bisexuality in men requires a contrast with bisexuality in women. This contrast, of course, reflects the importance of emphasizing the continuities of female sexuality among heterosexuals, homosexuals, and bisexuals, and the similar continuities of male sexuality across sex-object choice categories. This focus on gender differences would address the observed differences in romantic attachments to sex partners, the greater ability for women to be bisexual, the relative stigma attached to homosexual behavior in the two genders, and differential relationships between the psychology and physiology of sexual arousal and response.

NOTES

1. In this paper we are considering bisexuality only in men. Evidence of bisexuality in women is discussed, along with our own research in this area, in Blumstein and Schwartz (1976).

2. Hunt (1974) has argued that the Kinsey data presented an overestimation of the incidence of homosexual behavior among American males. While there is really no way to evaluate Hunt's assertion, it should be noted that studies published since the Kinsey original (including Hunt's) have contained flaws at least as serious as those in Kinsey's 1948 volume. Even if Hunt's data were trustworthy, they too show that the incidence of homosexual behavior is much greater than would be predicted from the number of persons who are nearly exclusively homosexual throughout their lives.

3. In a study of ten married Belgian homosexual males, Ross (1971) reported wide variation in the degree of sexual involvement between husband and wife. The reasons the author suggested for his respondents' initial decisions to marry include: failure to acknowledge their homosexuality prior to marriage; a "conscious flight from homosexuality"; choice of life goals that could be provided by heterosexual family life, e.g., children and companionship; and choice of a "conformist" home life necessary for career advancement or to meet the demands of relatives.

4. Such anonymous activities, often engaged in by bisexuals who would not frequent a gay bar, are not limited to restrooms, but are also found in some innercity movie houses, highway reststops, and numerous other locations (Troiden, 1974).

5. Tripp (1975) has offered the interesting observation that, although some men who pursue impersonal sexual relations (especially in public restrooms) claim they are seeking only an obliging orifice, they can be observed going to great lengths to locate the physically most attractive partner available.

6. It is important to note that a large number of homosexual males have had very limited heterosexual experience, and it is impossible to specify the variation in subjective reaction and subsequent reconstruction of those who are experienced. Saghir and Robins (1973) have estimated on the basis of 89 male and 57 female homosexuals (representative of no population in particular) that only 48% of the males, as contrasted with 79% of the females, had experienced heterosexual intercourse.

7. Perhaps this vision of the male homosexual community is overstated by our respondent. We do not mean to paint the gay community as a villain in thwarting a person's bisexuality. Indeed, our respondents were more inclined to report hostility toward, and disparagement of, their life styles among heterosexuals than among homosexuals, and some reported supportiveness for a bisexual orientation among homosexual friends.

8. Most of these respondents fell into our sample by responding to our advertisements for "persons with at least some sexual experience with men and women," posted in liberal churchs and community organizations.

REFERENCES

BLUMSTEIN, P. W. and P. SCHWARTZ (1976) "Bisexuality in women." Archives of Sexual Behavior 5 (March): 171-181.

GAGNON, J. H. and W. SIMON (1973) Sexual Conduct: The Social Sources of Human Sexuality. Chicago: Aldine.

HUMPHREYS, L. (1970) Tearoom Trade: Impersonal Sex in Public Restrooms. Chicago: Aldine.

HUNT, M. (1974) Sexual Behavior in the 1970's. Chicago: Playboy Press.

KINSEY, A. C., W. B. POMEROY, and C. E. MARTIN (1948) Sexual Behavior in the Human Male. Philadelphia: Saunders.

KIRKHAM, G. L. (1971) "Homosexuality in prison," pp. 325-349 in J. M. Henslin (ed.) Studies in the Sociology of Sex. New York: Appleton-Century-Crofts.

LINDER, R. (1948) "Sexual behavior in penal institutions," pp. 201-215 in A. Deutsch (ed.) Sex Habits of American Men. Englewood Cliffs, N.J.: Prentice-Hall.

REISS, A. J., Jr. (1961) "The social integration of queers and peers." Social Problems 9 (Fall): 102-120.

ROSS, H. L. (1971) "Modes of adjustment of married homosexuals." Social Problems 18 (Winter): 385-393.

SAGHIR, M. and E. ROBINS (1973) Male and Female Homosexuality. Baltimore: Williams & Wilkins.

SYKES, G. (1958) The Society of Captives. Princeton, N.J.: Princeton Univ. Press.

TRIPP, C. A. (1975) The Homosexual Matrix. New York: McGraw-Hill.

TROIDEN, R. R. (1974) "Homosexual encounters in a highway rest stop," pp. 211-228 in E. Goode and R. Troiden (eds.) Sexual Deviance and Sexual Deviants. New York: William Morrow.

WARREN, C.A.B. (1974) Identity and Community in the Gay World. New York: John Wiley.

WEINBERG, M. S. and C. J. WILLIAMS (1975) "Gay baths and the social organization of impersonal sex." Social Problems 23 (December): 124-136.

J. M. CARRIER is a member of the Gender Identity Research Clinic at UCLA.
Dr. Carrier is continuing his research on male homosexuality in Mexico and in
the Mexican-American community in Los Angeles.

FAMILY ATTITUDES AND
MEXICAN MALE HOMOSEXUALITY

J. M. CARRIER

LIVING WITH THE FAMILY of origin influences the sexual and
social activities of Mexican males who participate in homosexual encounters. At the time of the 1970 census, approximately 80% of single Mexican
males 20 years of age and older lived in some kind of family grouping.[1]
This statistic reflects the Mexican custom for individuals to continue to
live with their families as long as they are not married. Although many
may follow this custom because of insufficient income, the available
information suggests that even in the upper-income strata of the society a
majority continue to live with their families while single. The general belief
appears to be that should an individual want to leave the confines of the
family the only way of doing so, other than by marriage, is by moving to a
different city.

The census data also show that in 1970 about two-thirds of mestizoized
Mexican males in their early twenties, and one-third in their late twenties,

---

AUTHOR'S NOTE: An earlier version of this paper was presented at the first
annual meeting of the International Academy of Sex Research, Stony Brook,
New York, November 1975.

[99]

were not married.[2] The majority of these males live in Mexico City, other
large urban areas, and in the states of Northern Mexico.[3]

Thus, during the time that they are trying to meet the demands of a
high sexual need, single Mexican males must live at home and cope with
their family's attitudes and behavior toward sexuality. This paper
considers some of the ways in which family perspectives on homosexuality
appear to affect the behavior of those single Mexican males living at home
who utilize homosexual encounters as a significant or sole outlet for sexual
satisfaction.

DATA AND METHODS

The discussion in this paper is based mainly on beliefs about family and
societal attitudes toward homosexuality held by urban Mexican male
participants in homosexual encounters, and on the ways they claim to
behave—or have been observed to behave—in response to these beliefs.
Except for limited observations made by the author, data on attitudes
toward homosexuality of the parents and siblings or participants are not
available. Some general data on Mexican attitudes and behavior over time
are available from the various communication media, such as periodicals,
television, and movies.

The data on participants' beliefs and behavior were gathered by the
author during varying lengths of time spent in Mexico between the
summer of 1968 and the present. The longest period of observation was in
Guadalajara between fall 1969 and spring 1971. During this time period,
ten friendship circles and ten independent informants were socialized with,
and contacts were established with six families. The socioeconomic levels
of the families were as follows: two were in the poor, one in the
poor-in-transition, and three in the middle-solvent class.[4] During the latter
part of 1970 and early 1971, 53 respondents were interviewed (in Spanish)
in the city of Guadalajara. Observations have also been made in Mexico
City, Mazatlan, Guaymas, Chihuahua, Mexicali, Tijuana, and Ensenada.
(See Carrier, 1971, 1972, and 1976, for additional information on the
respondents and the questionnaire used in the structured interviews.)

At the time of interview, 88% (45 of 51) of the author's respondents in
Guadalajara were single and still living with their families. Of the six single
respondents not living with their families, two were orphaned when young;

one was an only child whose parents died when he was in his late teens; the families of two did not live in Guadalajara; and the family of one lives in Guadalajara. The latter respondent had to leave home at the age of 23 because he was no longer willing to obey his father's 10 p.m. curfew on weekday nights. The median age of of the single respondents is 22.

MEXICAN ATTITUDES TOWARD HOMOSEXUALITY

Judging from the behavior and beliefs of the author's informants in Mexico, from the views presented in Mexican newspapers, magazines, television programs, and motion pictures, and from the operations of the Mexican law authorities, we can see the general public in Mexico tends to view homosexuality with considerable disapproval. On the surface their view does not appear to differ from the cultural view held by a majority of North Americans that homosexuality is both sick and shameful.

In reply to a question about social attitudes, a large majority of the Guadalajaran respondents (42 of 48) stated that they believed most people in Guadalajara had strong negative feelings about males who have continuing sexual relationships with other males. Among the majority opinions, three adjectives were used by 45% of the respondents (19 of 42) to describe social attitudes toward homosexuality: bad (n = 10), repugnant (n = 6), and immoral (n = 3). Other words used were: contrary, disgusting, dislike, disapproving, scandalous, rejecting, nonaccepting, censorable, against, cannot stand, negatively, afraid, concerned, puritanical, and hypocritical.

The following illustrates the kind of responses made by informants:

–The people of Guadalajara will never accept us because they have a bad idea about homosexuals . . . the worst idea . . . but when they get to know us they accept it because they get to understand us.

–The majority of the people believe that it is terrible . . . very bad . . . and that we ought not to exist.

–Half of the people repudiate this kind of behavior. Of the other half: some are indifferent; for others it is interesting; others accept it . . . especially the amoral; and yet others accept it for a variety of reasons.

–The people are hypocrites. They talk only to talk because in every family there are one or two *activos* or *pasivos*.

Although not a taboo subject, the homosexual male is either handled as a joke or is ridiculed and condemned in the mass media in Mexico; an association is almost always made between effeminacy and homosexuality. For example, the most popular variety show on Mexican television, *Siempre Domingos,* often presents skits which depict certain males as weak, passive, and effeminate—and thus by inference homosexual. The same general theme is also presented in the stage shows of a popular variety theater in Guadalajara and in night clubs located in the *zona roja* of many urban areas. Homosexual characters in Mexican movies are similarly portrayed as effeminate. *Los Superfrios,* a popular Mexican comic book series, devoted an issue to the story of a Mexican general and his attempts to interest his effeminate son in girls (Los Superfrios, 1970). A popular Mexican magazine recently had a cover story using material from a *Time* magazine feature on homosexuality in the United States (Sucesos, 1975). However, instead of having a masculine Air Force sergeant on the cover as did *Time,* they had an effeminate man with limp wrists seated cross-legged in a chair and dressed in a turn-of-the-century suit and shirt with ruffled sleeves. He was seated under a large, pink banner headline: "Soy Homosexual" (I am a homosexual). In Mexican novels, homosexuality is presented as a tortuous, agonizing experience (e.g., Maldonado, 1969).

The most denigrating view of homosexuality in the mass media is given by a widely read tabloid newspaper published every Wednesday in Mexico City and distributed throughout Mexico. Called *ALARMA!*, it focuses on grisly murders, rapes, scandals, and highway accidents occurring all over Mexico. During the year and a half I read the publication, it contained considerable reporting about homosexual activity in Mexico and the United States, and at least once a month it had a banner headline about homosexuals. In their headlines and reportage the same general viewpoint was usually maintained, namely, that homosexual males are degenerate, vicious, immoral, and effeminate. Another tabloid newspaper, *Alerta,* presents essentially the same picture but has counterbalanced it somewhat since 1974 with a relatively sympathetic view in a weekly column titled: "Anatomia Del Homosexual."

The following headlines are representative of *ALARMA!* from November 1969 to the present.

(1) June 10, 1970—"Epidemia de Desviados Sexuales" (Rash of Sexual Deviates)

(2) December 16, 1970—"Asquerosa Depravacion Sexual" (Disgusting Sexual Depravity)

(3) March 10, 1971—"Furor de Sexos Equivacados en la Immoralidad Del Carnival" (Madness of Female Impersonators in the Immorality of the Mardi Gras)

(4) July 7, 1971—"Atrevimiento de Degenerados! Boda de dos Homosexuales!" (Boldness of Degenerates! Marriage of Two Homosexuals!)

(5) October 1, 1975—"Degenerados "Mujercitos" Venden Amor y Sucias Caricias!" (Degenerate "girl-boys" sell love and dirty caresses!)

(6) June 2, 1976—"Fichaban en Cabarets; Los Mujercitos" (Boy-girls were cruising in night clubs!)

Each of the headlines was accompanied by photographs of effeminate males or males dressed in female clothes, and by text on the cover or inside the periodical which tersely described the kind of activity to be expected from homosexual males—that is, lewd, repulsive, and bizarre. Attempts were often made to lead the reader to believe it commonplace that homosexuals were involved with murder, robbery, drugs, and other types of criminal activities. The link with criminality has also been made by the Mexican president. In a nationwide address in September 1974, he noted that among other things in the background of members of terrorist groups there is "a high incidence of masculine and feminine homosexuality" (Fourth State of the Nation Report, 1974).

Although there are no legal sanctions in Mexico against consenting adult males having sexual relations in private, every effort is made by the law authorities to keep behavior which by their definition might be interpretable as homosexual (i.e., effeminate or "campy" behavior) as invisible as possible to the general public. Both uniformed and plain-clothed policemen are used to enforce this policy. The police are most active in parks and movie houses where they harass and/or arrest offending males to suppress open solicitation as much as possible. They also close down or force a policy change in steam bath houses that have a scandalous reputation for homosexual activity and are thus known to the population at large.

Counterposed to Mexican society's generally disapproving attitude toward homosexuality is the fact that people appear to accept the inevitability of homosexual contacts between men. There seems to be a wide acceptance of the reality that most males have multiple sexual outlets when single and have sexual outlets over and above those provided by the wife when married. Although not socially approved, these extramarital outlets are nevertheless generally accepted as long as they are carried out with a certain amount of discretion. Homosexual contacts between males are thought no better or worse than other kinds of sexual outlets that do not carry social approval. This understanding, however, is essentially extended only to those playing the insertor sex role. Masculine males who play the "active" insertor role in homosexual encounters are not generally conceptualized as homosexuals in Mexico unless they become overly involved or utilize this sexual outlet exclusively.

FAMILY ATTITUDES AND BEHAVIOR

Almost three-fourths of the respondents with family connections (36 of 49) believed their feelings about having sex with another male were affected in some way by family attitudes and behavior; one-third of the total (16 of 49) felt they were affected a great deal. The major feeling they said they had to cope with was their family's general attitude of shame toward homosexuals. The following illustrates the kind of shame felt by respondents:

  —They (the family) must know . . . but I go on pretending I'm interested in girls. I don't think about it too much but I'm ashamed about some of my feminine ways, and how my parents must feel about me. It's such a disgrace to have a *joto* in the family.

  —At times I feel so ashamed. My mother talks of marriage. . . . I don't want to get married. I get more and more involved with men. I worry over what's going to happen. Maybe I should get married!

  —I know my father worries about me being one of those on the other side. If he ever finds out for sure I'll leave. I can't remember a time when he wasn't talking about the importance of having balls . . . and marrying and having a family.

As a result of family attitudes, a majority of the respondents expressed concern over how much their parents and siblings knew about their homosexuality. Close to two-thirds said they definitely did not want their families to know. And even though one parent or sibling might know or suspect, they still felt the need to hide the behavior from the unknowing or unsuspecting family members. In response to a question of how frequently they were concerned about the possibility of being found out by unknowing or unsuspecting family members, a large majority (34 of 43) replied they were concerned at least occasionally; and 42% (18 of 43) said it was something they had experienced anxiety about frequently.

Knowledge about homosexually behaving sons and brothers in Mexico appears to vary among family members. More brothers, sisters, and cousins of respondents, for example, knew than parents; more mothers knew than fathers. A majority (57%) of the respondents believed that no one in their family knew for sure. One-third felt that they were reasonably sure their mothers at least suspected. Fewer (about 16%) held this same belief about their fathers. Table 1 presents respondents' beliefs about family knowledge of their homosexuality.

Coping With Family

The homosexually involved Mexican male, still single and living with his family, must cope over time with the dissonance generated by his behavior and the family's negative view of the homosexual as a shameful being. Given that a major strategy appears to be concealment, the most important part of coping is concerned with categorizing behavior as acceptable or unacceptable insofar as it might result in exposing the involved male to his family. The verb *quemar* is generally used in conversation in Mexico to label behavior considered unacceptable. Quemar literally means to burn or scorch. Reference is thus made to the fact that one's reputation may be burnt or scorched by a revealing bit of behavior.

The two situations most feared by Mexican males involved in homosexual encounters are (1) to be seen in the company of, or acknowledged by, males judged effeminate and thus by implication homosexual, and (2) to be seen going into or leaving a place where homosexuals are known to congregate. In the early days of the study in Guadalajara, the author unwittingly put a number of respondents in extremely tense situations by not understanding this apprehension and

TABLE 1
Family Knowledge about
Respondents' Homosexuality

Family Knowledge	Mother	Father	Other[a]
Know	21%	15%	43%
Suspect	31%	16%	
Neither know nor suspect	48%	69%	
Sample No.	48	39	51

a. Respondents' were only asked whether "other" family members knew about their homosexuality, so the distribution of knowledge between the other two categories is not available.

fear. For example, while walking down a main boulevard in Guadalajara early one evening with a respondent who judged himself quite masculine, the author stopped and engaged in a brief conversation with an effeminate respondent coming from the opposite direction. Before the author could make an introduction, the masculine respondent quickly walked a short distance away to dissociate himself. This respondent explained later that in such a public location he was afraid of being seem by relatives talking to such an obvious homosexual. He concluded his explanation by saying: "El me quema!" (literally: he, the feminine male, burns my reputation).

The fear of being seen going into a place identified with homosexuals by relatives causes many males to limit their attendance. For example, a majority of the author's respondents in Guadalajara only occasionally (and a sizeable number never) patronized the two bars which catered to homosexuals. It is relevant to note that even in the largest urban areas in Mexico, including Mexico City, there are usually only one or two "gay" bars; and they have an exclusively homosexual clientele only at night. Although the closing of these establishments by law authorities (except perhaps for a favored few) is a recurring pattern, reluctance to enter alone would probably limit their number. It is difficult to imagine any Mexican city having the number of exclusively homosexual establishments that are found in major cities in the United States.

Another aspect of coping is activity which may be carried out to divert attention from homosexual involvement. Social contacts with girlfriends and heterosexual intercourse with prostitutes, for example, may be maintained as a cover. And any masculine-type activity may be used on a routine basis to promote a heterosexual image. The Latin custom of paying a great deal of attention to a passing girl by whistling or making remarks, for instance, may be as avidly carried out by a homosexually involved male as by a heterosexually involved one.

The level of activity required for family coping appears to depend for the most part on the degree of involvement in homosexual encounters and on the relative effeminacy or masculinity of the individual.

Individuals heavily involved in homosexual encounters structure their social life differently from less involved males. The greater the involvement, the greater the need for defenses and covering activities within the family. To sustain a large number of different sexual outlets, for example, they must spend proportionately more time hiding the activity from the family. Those males maintaining a relationship with only one partner also carry a proportionately heavier burden since they must create a cover for the time spent socializing with the lover.

Exclusively homosexual males, the available data suggest, spend most of their free time—that is, time away from family, work, and/or school—socializing with homosexual friends. Because a large majority continue to live with their families, however, social activity is limited by family functions and parental rules and regulations. For example, a usual regulation is that each night he must return home to sleep; generally he must return home at specific hours or face the anger or scolding of parents. This even includes those males in their late twenties and thirties. For instance, two respondents in Guadalajara who were 28 years old and lovers earned sufficient income to rent their own apartment; but only one of the two, whose family lived in another city, was able to live in full time. His lover, still living with his family, was limited to occasional overnight visits.

Most of the above restrictions continue to apply to individuals even though their homosexual behavior may have been revealed to all members of the family. A major coping strategy for both sides is to act as though the behavior is not taking place, i.e., there is a "conspiracy of silence" or "counterfeit secrecy" (see also Ponse, this issue). The homosexually involved individuals thus continue to act in such a way that they do not expose themselves to unknowing relatives, neighbors, or friends. They may continue to maintain the fiction, for example, that some day they will marry and have children; and social occasions at the house may be organized as though their interests were heterosexual.

A Limited Subculture

The combination of family demands and the need to conceal the stigmatizing behavior from the family has created a set of circumstances which in part has limited the development of homosexual subcultures in even the largest Mexican cities. The family grasp on single male members, for example, essentially precludes the sharing of apartments by male friends and the setting up of households by homosexual lovers. "Gay ghettos" of the type that exist in San Francisco and Los Angeles are thus not found in Mexico. And, as previously noted, the number of exclusive meeting places is limited by the concept of "quemado" and by the law authorities. There are usually only one or two gay bars. To the author's knowledge, there are no exclusively homosexual steam baths in Mexico. The homosexual activity which does take place in steam baths, of which there are a large number, is generally covert. The management and/or law authorities continuously exert pressure to limit such behavior.

Homosexual "cruising" patterns also appear to be determined in part by family controls. Both the hours and the locations of cruising, for example, are limited by fears of being found out and by the need to adhere to parental rules and regulations for returning home at night and by a given hour. Thus even on weekends, cruising appears to occur more often in the late afternoon or early evening rather than late evening. And it more often takes place in relatively anonymous locations such as the dark upper balconies of move theaters and parks, rather than in exposed or known places.

Effeminate Family Members

Given the cultural norms equating effeminacy and homosexuality in Mexico, homosexually involved effeminate males must contend with a different set of family responses than involved masculine males. Suspicions about individuals being homosexual as a result of effeminate behavior start at an early age in Mexican families. Great importance is thus attached to manly behavior in young boys. Villasenor (1964), for example, found that 94 of the 100 middle-class mothers making up her sample believed it important for a boy "to be manly." Penalosa (1968), after reviewing all the available literature on the Mexican family, concludes: "Any signs of feminization are severely repressed in the boy." Scolding of nonmanly behavior in young boys, is less likely to take the form of "act like a man" than the form of "don't act like a *maricon, puto,* or *joto.*" In addition to designating a male effeminate these terms also designate him as a male who likes to play the anal insertee ("passive") role.

Adolescent males are also pressured while in their early teens, (often at the first signs of puberty) by their brothers, male cousins, and/or friends to prove their masculinity by having intercourse with prostitutes or available neighborhood girls. The Guadalajara data show, for example, that a majority of the respondents rating themselves as average or very masculine in early adolescence (18 of 20) had heterosexual intercourse between the ages of 14 and 18; the median age being 16. And, about one-third of those respondents rating themselves slightly or very effeminate (7 of 22) reported they had also tried heterosexual intercourse under pressure of peers or relatives.

Effeminate males in the mestizoized segment of the Mexican population eventually, if not from the beginning, move toward exclusively homosexual behavior. There is considerable evidence that males unable to live up to family and cultural expectations of manly behavior accept their effeminacy and play an overtly homosexual role. There is also some evidence suggesting that families may make an accommodation with the effeminate member. For several respondents it took the following general form. The father gave up trying to have any influence on the behavior of the effeminate son who interacted mainly with his mother and sisters. The tactic most often used by the father was to ignore the presence of the effeminate son and to focus his interest on his other sons.[5] As one very effeminate 22-year-old respondent reported: "My father never talks to me. . . . He is always polite to my friends when they come to play bingo on Sundays but he leaves the house as soon as they get in. I like it that way." The author observed this father's behavior on a number of occasions. He talked to the author at great length and to his other sons, but not once was he observed interacting with his effeminate son. When the respondent and his effeminate friends started playing bingo with his mother and sisters, his father and brothers would always leave the house. Another general aspect of family behavior is that the effeminate brother develops an alliance with an older sister, usually the eldest, who acts as a buffer between her brother and the male members of the family. The most striking relationship of this type observed in Guadalajara was between a 21-year-old effeminate respondent, the youngest of nineteen children, and his 30-year-old sister. She had separated from her husband and returned home with her four children to live. She defended her effeminate brother against both the father and the hostile older brothers—all married except one. In addition, she and her effeminate brother essentially exchanged traditional roles. She worked six days a week in a factory. He stayed home and helped their mother take care of the children and do the washing, ironing, and cooking.

The Effeminate Male Target

Another aspect of family behavior affecting male homosexuality is that from an early age onward effeminate males in Mexico are sexual targets for other males. All but one of the author's respondents scoring on the effeminate side as a child (17 of 18) had sexual contacts with older postpubertal males prior to their first ejaculation; 13 of the 17 had contacts between 5 and 10 years of age.[6] In comparison, as shown by Table 2, only 9 of 29 males scoring on the masculine side had sexual contacts with postpubertal males prior to their first ejaculation. The encounters reported were more than a casual one-time sexual experience for most of the respondents. A majority (21 of 26) had on different occasions two or more sexual experiences with their older male partners; six had continuous sexual experiences with the same partner for one year or longer.

Following the onset of puberty, effeminate males continue to be sexual targets for other males because of their effeminacy. The consensus of the effeminate respondents in Guadalajara is that regardless of whether they are at school, in a movie theater, on the downtown streets, in a park, or in their own neighborhood, they are sought out and expected to play the anal insertee sex role by more masculine males. As one 14-year-old respondent answered the question of where he looked for sexual contacts during the year prior to interview, "I didn't have to search for them . . . they looked for me (ellos me buscan a mi)."

Another aspect of the effeminate male as a sexual target is that many early homosexual encounters, judging from the available data, are carried out with relatives and friends of the family. This appears to be particularly true for the preadolescent effeminate male. Of the adult contacts 36% were relatives; 46% were friends and/or neighbors. Only 18% were strangers. Several of the prepubertal homosexual contacts with relatives, it is interesting to note, were maintained over extended periods of time. For example, one respondent had a weekly sexual relationship with a cousin for about four years. He was eight and his cousin fifteen at the start of the relationship. Another respondent had a weekly sexual relationship with his

TABLE 2
**Comparison of Respondents' Effeminacy Scores
as a Child and Prepubertal Homosexual Contacts
with Postpubertal Males[a]**

| | | Sexual Contact with Postpubertal Male Prior to First Ejaculation | | |
		Yes	No	Total
Effeminacy	High	17	1	18
Score	Low	9	20	29
	Total	26	21	47

a. The adjusted "phi coefficient" is equal to .87. $X^2 = 18.07$, (1 df, $P > 0.001$).

uncle for two years. He was ten when the relationship started, his uncle eighteen. Both relationships were terminated by the younger partners when the older relative married.

Homosexual relationships between effeminate males and their relatives appear to taper off by the end of the early teens of the effeminate males. Some postadolescent sexual contacts with relatives do continue, however, particularly with cousins. One respondent from a small farming community located a short distance from Guadalajara reported a network of sexual relationships between himself, two uncles, and five cousins. At the time of interview (at age 23), he said that the relationships were still active but only infrequently carried out. A relatively effeminate male, he also said that as far as he knew the relatives were only homosexually active with him—not with each other. He played the anal insertee sex role. Only two effeminate respondents reported sexual relations with their brothers; both played the anal insertee role.

Masculine Family Members

Homosexually involved masculine Mexican males obviously face a different set of family responses than do involved effeminate ones. They are not as easily identified as "homosexual" as are feminine males; and, if they only play the active insertor sex role and are not exclusively involved, they are not stigmatized to the same degree. They still do not want their parents or siblings to know about their homosexual behavior, however. It might be acceptable to talk about their homosexual outlets to friends at school and/or work, but never with members of the family. Table 3 shows that a much higher percentage of the parents of respondents who preferred to play only the anal insertor role—a predominantly masculine group of respondents—neither knew nor suspected that their sons were homosexually involved.

Masculine family members having extensive homosexual outlets over time are much more concerned about being exposed as a homosexual than are their effeminate male counterparts in other families.[7] As a consequence, they must spend more time worrying about avoiding situations which might "burn" or "scorch" their reputation. The masculine Mexican males who face the greatest amount of dissonance in their lives, however, are those who in addition to being homosexually involved also play the anal insertee sex role. They must worry about exposure and contend with the role conflict generated by being masculine and playing the female role.

TABLE 3
Knowledge of Parents about Respondents'
Homosexuality Compared by Sex Role Played[a]

Parental Knowledge	Sex Role Played				Total[b]	
	Insertor		Insertee			
	Mo	Fa	Mo	Fa	Mo	Fa
Know	10%	7%	37%	27%	21%	15%
Suspect	25%	7%	37%	20%	31%	16%
Neither know nor suspect	65%	86%	26%	53%	48%	69%
Sample No.	20	15	19	15	48	39

a. First sustained year of homosexual activity following first ejaculation.
b. The total includes those respondents who played both the insertor and insertee sex roles.

The Guadalajara data suggest that most masculine males playing the anal insertee role start out first playing only the anal insertor role. As they become more and more involved in homosexual encounters, they experiment with the anal insertee role and begin incorporating it into their sexual repertoire. An interesting aspect of their behavior is that they generally are not willing to play the insertee role with a male judged less masculine than themselves.

The masculine male faces the problem of effeminacy only in that he may worry whether or not his public image is masculine enough. His principal family problem is more likely to be connected with the implications of being single and the amount of interest he is able to display in females and marriage. The more involved he is in homosexual encounters, the more intense the problem. If he also vacillates between sex roles, he adds the burden of self-contempt for his passivity. As long as he can remember he has been taught to act like a man, not like a "joto," "puto," or "maricon." All his problems deepen as he grows older and still finds it necessary or wants to live with his family.

The kind of tense family situation a masculine male faces is illustrated by the following family conversation heard by the author during the birthday lunch of a very masculine respondent:

After finishing our meal the dishes were cleared and the women left. The conversation drifted to sports, automobiles, and jokes about driving. The father then started talking about *jotos* by first telling a joke about the governor of the State. He slowly explained to me that the governor is *soltero* (single) and *dicen* (they say) he is a *joto*. The father talked next about the carnival in Veracruz and the men who went out on the streets dressed as women. He talked about all these things in a very jovial manner. Memo (the respondent) and his younger friend listened and laughed but said nothing. A friend of the father made a few comments about *afeminados* (effeminate males) in Tokyo and then the subject was changed. Throughout the conversation Memo appeared not only exceptionally quiet but also exceptionally nervous!

For those males who feel that their families at most only suspect or who believe that their families know nothing at all there is the uncertainty of what will happen to them if they are found out. One of the greatest fears expressed by many is that they will have to leave their family home. This may be by choice because of the shame associated with their homosexual behavior or it may be by an edict from their father. In either event, the outcome may be the same: the leaving of home and ensuing alienation from family. There is insufficient data to make even a preliminary conclusion about how often this fear of being cast out is realized. It does happen—a masculine respondent was forced to leave home by his father after his homosexuality had been uncovered. But this may be the exception rather than the rule. As shown by Table 3, a number of respondents were known to be homosexual by both parents, and yet they had not been forced to leave home.

DISCUSSION

Because there are only limited data available on the Mexican family and male homosexual behavior, conclusions based on the data must be considered preliminary. Given the family grasp on single males and the relatively late age at marriage, however, it seems clear that the attitudes and behavior of the mestizoized Mexican family toward homosexuality play an important role in shaping the behavior of family members who are homosexually active. The ways in which homosexual behavior is affected by the family appear to depend both on the relative effeminacy or masculinity of the involved individual and on his preference for playing the insertor or insertee sex role.

It also seems clear that the lack of a developed homosexual subculture in Mexico is in part due to family influences. The Mexican family thus appears to play a far more important role with respect to the structure of homosexual behavior than does the middle-class Anglo-American family.

NOTES

1. This percentage was derived by dividing the number of males living alone (*personas solas, hombres*) by the number of single males (*personas solteros, hombres*) 20 years of age and older. The census data are from Resumen General Abreviado (1972).

2. Mestizos are Mexican nationals of mixed Indian and Spanish ancestry. They make up a large majority of the population, and their culture is the dominant one.

3. A majority of the population in the southern Mexican states continues to be influenced by Indian cultures. One result of this appears to be the marriage of males at an earlier age than in mestizoized areas. In this paper only the behavior of mestizoized Mexican males is considered. See Carrier (1976) for a detailed examination of the census data.

4. The socioeconomic classes, originated by Leyva (1969), are based on monthly average family income per capita: (1965 pesos) poor-155, poor-in-transition-223, middle-insolvent-326, and middle-solvent-504. The current exchange rate is 12.5 pesos = 1 dollar U.S.

5. It is important to note that a large majority of the effeminate respondents (20 of 22) came from large families with more brothers on the average than sisters. Additionally, a large majority (18 of 22) were raised in households with both natural parents present.

6. The following criteria are used as indicators of preadolescent effeminacy: remembered self as effeminate, played with dolls, cross-dressed one or more times, experienced desire at least once to be female, and had little or no interest in sports. Eighteen respondents received a high effeminacy score using these criteria.

7. It is the degree of homosexual involvement that appears to be important. Masculine males who predominantly or exclusively choose homosexual outlets may not be as severely stigmatized as are effeminate males but their behavior may be censured nevertheless.

REFERENCES

CARRIER, J. M. (1976) "Cultural factors affecting urban Mexican male homosexual behavior." Archives of Sexual Behavior 5, 2: 103-124.

––– (1972) "Urban Mexican male homosexual encounters: an analysis of participants and coping strategies." Ph.D. dissertation, University of California, Irvine.

––– (1971) "Participants in urban Mexican male homosexual encounters." Archives of Sexual Behavior 1, 4: 279-291.

Fourth State of the Nation Report (1974) Separata: Mexican Newsletter 21 (September 1): 5

LEYVA, J. (1970) "El problema habitacional," in El Perfil de Mexico en 1980. Vol. 2. Mexico, D.F.: Siglo XXI Editores, S.A.

Los Superfrios (1970) "El Generalote," p. 120.

MALDONADO, J. C. (1969) Despues De Todo. Mexico, D.F.: Editorial Diogenes, S.A.

PENALOSA, F. (1968) "Mexican family roles." J. of Marriage and the Family 30: 680-689.

Resumen General Abreviado (1972) IX Censo General de Poblacion.

Sucesos (1975) "Homosexualismo." Mexico, D.F.: 107 Col. Polanco. 2-10.

VILLASENOR, I. (1964) "El Mexicano: la familia." Ph.D. dissertation. University of Guadalajara.

SHARON KANTOROWSKI DAVIS is a doctoral student in Sociology at the University of Southern California. She is a coauthor of *Social Problems of the Seventies.* Currently she is applying the dramaturgical approach to the study of the family.

PHILLIP W. DAVIS is a Lecturer at the University of California, Riverside. He is completing a study of order maintenance strategies used by police.

MEANINGS AND PROCESS
IN EROTIC OFFENSIVENESS

An Expose of Exposees

SHARON KANTOROWSKI DAVIS
PHILLIP W. DAVIS

EROTIC OFFENSIVENESS and sexual victimization have been studied primarily as instances of collective action taken by groups in response to "offensive" conditions such as pornography (see, for example, Zurcher et al., 1971), or as instances of forceful assaults upon the victim's physical person. The presumption has been that offensiveness and victimization are best understood by examining the characteristics of the offenders. Our concern here, however, is with a type of erotic offensiveness and victimization from the perspective of those who are accosted and presumably offended. More specifically, we will be concerned with the reactions of women who have encountered male strangers engaging in what is most often referred to in lay, psychiatric, and legal parlance as "exhibitionism" or "indecent exposure."[1]

[117]

The more psychodynamic depictions of exhibitionism have tended to view the act primarily in unilateral terms by examining the biographies, sexual histories, motives, and intelligence of the exhibitionist. He has been variously charged with epilepsy, depravity, psychoses, neuroses, neurasthenia, idiocy, sadism, and sometimes simply with "adventurousness." What is uniformly missing from these earlier examinations of exhibitionism, however, is an interest in the meanings of the experience for the women designated as "victims." The victim's perceptions and reactions have been of concern only to the extent that they are thought to either gratify or frustrate the exhibitionist's desire for a conventionally "shocked" reaction.[2] We learn only that the greater the reaction of the victim the greater the sexual gratification of the exhibitionist.

PERSPECTIVE AND METHOD

It has been suggested that actors who frequent public places are by definition moving through a somewhat distinct social space which carries with it a diversity of social meanings and rules of order. These meanings and rules provide the interpretive backdrop or set of understandings in light of which the untoward and the unexpected take on their meaning, are handled or managed, and are accounted for. Moreover, part of that public urban order is founded upon rules which concern the appropriate overtures by which strangers may initiate and perhaps continue an engagement (Goffman, 1963: 124). This discussion of reactions[3] to exposures will devote itself to the analysis of situations where social actors have encountered or have been approached by accosting alters in an untoward fashion where alter was likely to be of a disreputable moral character and neglectful of the rules which govern or guide more civil overtures.[4]

Believing that a more grounded and descriptive approach to sexual offensiveness and victimization is needed, we conducted depth interviews with 25 women who were generally young, middle-class, Caucasian adults with some college education.[5] They volunteered on a self-selecting basis as having "encountered an exhibitionist." The definitional question thus in part was left to the interviewee and was knowingly begged in that we thought it important to discover the range of phenomena that urban actors might dub exhibitionism. Since many of those interviewed described more than one such incident, access to over 40 incidents of "exposure" was gained. Clearly, our analysis is rooted in the retrospective views[6] of actors who define themselves as having been "exposed to" and will have nothing to say about the beliefs, desires, emotions, and mental states of the people who expose themselves.[7] It is assumed that these interview data have fallen heir to the many difficulties and limitations surrounding retrospective data. The fact that we seem to have a large incidence of what Gagnon (1965) has termed "multiple accidental victims" could suggest a bias toward a normalization or "acceptance" of the phenomenon which might have led to the voluntary self-reportage. Similarly it is possible that those who have had the experience at least once are more likely to define themselves as having experienced it time and again. We will attempt to describe the meanings of the experience by discussing the range of emotional, definitional, and strategic reactions generated by and used to deal with this type of trouble.

EMOTIONS AND STRATEGIES
IN THE ENCOUNTER

The sociology of erotic offensiveness (see Kirkpatrick and Kanin, 1957) and accosting behavior must necessarily examine the ways in which those who have been accosted experience and define the encounter. When boldly confronted by someone who has neglected the normatively established modes of staging overtures to open and extend engagements with a stranger, we might expect the person confronted to react in a somewhat outraged fashion. The emotional reactions among our interviewees do not support this imagery.[8] While most interviewees said they were nervous, scared, or afraid in the situation and in two cases "hysterical," the intensity of the affective reactions was reported to be far less than we expected. Although some reported a sense of being "offended" or outraged, fear and surprise were the more common reactions.

In discussing "engagements among the unacquainted," Goffman (1963: 143) has suggested that in the instance of exhibitionism,

the communication structure of the event often consists of an individual initiating an engagement with a stranger of the opposite sex by means of the kind of message that would be proper only if they were on close and intimate terms. Apart from psychodynamic issues, exhibitionists often *spectacularly* subvert the protective social control that keeps individuals interpersonally distant even though they are physically close to each other. The assault here is not so much directly on an individual as on the system of rights and symbols the individual employs in expressing relatedness and unrelatedness to those about him [emphasis added].

We will be concerned throughout with this "spectacular subversion" of the rules of public order by the erotically accosting type of agent known as the exhibitionist. It will be seen that the concern of the interviewee was less with the interpretation of "relatedness" or social closeness which might be inferred from the genital display and more with the practical matters of whether or not to "do something" and how to make sense of the encounter.

In this section we will first discuss the interviewees' sense of the accidental or fated nature of the encounter. We will emphasize the importance of the situational context in shaping the social meanings given to the experience. The interviewee's affective reactions to and ways of dealing with the erotically accosting encounter can be seen to center on the three strategic axes of getting away, getting help, and getting involved.

It Happened to Happen

Of recent concern in the study of untoward or criminal behavior has been the special vulnerabilities of victims by virtue of their age, race, and sexual status. Our concern here, however, is with the victim's *own* sense of the reasons behind her personal or *particular* victimization and if she defined herself to have been discriminately singled out. Some women thought that the exposer must have simply been waiting—not for them in particular—but rather for "just anyone," or just any woman or girl at all. Thus by virtue of being female, many of the interviewees felt especially "open" (Goffman, 1963) to this encounter and that they had been singled out by the exposer only by virtue of their sexual status and by the fact that they had "happened by." The fact that they and not others had become part of the encounter did not seem to bother or puzzle the interviewees. The untoward alter had not, in a sense, chosen them in particular but rather had approached them through circumstances over which the interviewees felt they had no control. The encounter happened to happen—largely because they were "just women" who were "just there" or who "just happened by."

> I feel that it was coincidental: I was there. It wasn't like he was following us. For all I know he might have been going around and flashing at everyone. He might have done it 20 times a day.

> I thought it was strictly because I was sitting on the bench and happened to be there and he happened to be around there. He *could* have been hiding, if he had this purpose, or he just happened to be there, and I happened to be there. . . . Maybe the reason he did that (was) he just happened to see me (and thought), "there's a girl."

In addition to viewing the encounter as essentially by chance, some interviewees thought that they became involved in the encounter because the exposer possessed a set of seemingly esoteric criteria or requirements which, while essentially unknown to them, to some degree might explain their particular involvement.

> It was a large group of girls and there were other clusters—they were spread out. I don't know why we were picked, maybe because there were a lot of girls together (they were walking home from school in a group). It was an *opportune time* [emphasis added].

> There were other places around, with people around, but I was sitting in the middle of the wall. *Maybe it was a good location for him,* . . . because he didn't say anything to me and it was like I wasn't even there [emphasis added].

> I would think that would be *the most convenient place* for him to stop. We had a good view, and there was no one sitting out there, no men around. And it was convenient for him [emphasis added].

This suggests that public places are viewed as settings in which virtually any female urban actor *could become* vulnerable to accosting advances. Certain accosting actors are clearly viewed as essentially nonselective or if viewed as selective, their criteria are esoteric and do not require a particular victim or object.

Getting Away

In most instances of exposure the interviewees sought to *remove* or *distance* themselves from the encounter. Removal might simply be a technique of avoidance and neglect, or a means of physically removing themselves from the immediate vicinity of the exhibitionist. "Getting away" then refers to the strategy of neglect as well as physical egress from the encounter. The three aspects of getting away to be considered are (1) instances where the encounter seemed to terminate itself; (2) instances where the interviewee avoided the encounter or tried to lessen its implications while still remaining within the immediate vicinity; and (3) instances where the interviewee attempted physical egress. These aspects will be considered in turn coupled with an attempt to retain the context of emotions and definitions as they were described to us.

OVER AND DONE WITH

Because of the specific settings in which some exposures occurred and because of the activities in which one or both of the parties were already engaged, the accosted party neither faced a situation which seemed to require deliberate steps to be taken nor was placed in a position of deciding how to extricate herself socially or spatially from the encounter. Here distance from the encounter seems to occur almost mechanically.

With moving vehicles, for example, the exposure is at times over of its own accord. In one instance, bicyclists were moving quickly around a blind turn on a bikepath in opposite directions and had visual access but momentarily. In such cases both parties, should they continue with actions already in progress, can be far apart after only a relatively short period of time.

> I was pedaling on a bikeway when a young adult male came breezing down a dip in the bikeway from the opposite direction. As he passed she saw that the crotch of his gym shorts had been torn out and he was fully exposed. He smiled and said something like, "whee" as he passed quickly by.

In another instance two women continued pedaling past the person exposing himself.

> My girlfriend and I, we took our bikes to the bike trail. We were just riding back, and we were talking and stuff. This dumb kid, he was about fourteen, went around us, and rode clear up the trail a little ways, and jumped off his bike. I thought God, what's he going to do now, knock over our bikes or something. As we rode by he dropped his drawers right there, and he was saying all this stuff. And Janie just got scared to death. I didn't see anything wrong with it because, I figured, you know guys when they're about fourteen go through all these stages.

Because of the wealth of cues of an apparent commitment by both parties to adhere to the main involvement (Goffman, 1963) (e.g., pedaling and driving in their appropriate settings) there may be reactions of puzzlement and surprise but little speculation as to a morbid intent behind the exposure.

In instances where the interviewee and exposer were walking in opposite directions with the interviewee having no warning, she may be left only with the feeling of surprise.

> A friend and I were by ourselves, it was daytime and there weren't many people on the street, but it was a busy part of the city. He was just passing and as he passed he just dropped his pants and whipped out his penis and kept on walking. I thought, "oh." It happened so fast that it wasn't a threat. He didn't stop. He kept on with his pace. He was walking leisurely. He unzipped his fly and dropped his pants a little bit, not down to his knees. It happened very quickly. There was no warning and nothing to make me be afraid.

Where there are signs available that the exhibitionist remains "engaged" within the situation and committed to an otherwise main involvement, there appears to be less fear in the affective reactions of our interviewees and less speculation that he poses an immediate threat.

WELL STUDIED NEGLECT

Goffman (1963: 83-88) has defined civil inattention as the process whereby one person may

> treat others as if they were not there at all, as objects not worthy of a glance, let alone close scrutiny . . . while . . . withdrawing one's attention from him so as to express that he does not constitute a target of special curiosity or design. . . . By according civil inattention, the individual implies that he has no reason to fear the others, be hostile to them, or wish to avoid them.

Civil inattention when employed in dealing with the exhibitionist may take the form of trying to ignore the untoward act by looking away, diverting one's gaze, or in other ways not paying attention to him.

> I was up in the library at a desk . . . and I was really busy. And this fellow comes and sat down on the floor . . . leaning against my desk, more or less with his legs out into the aisle, more or less touching the stacks of books, and started masturbating. And I saw that I got scared, but it really didn't scare me that much. But I didn't want to get up and move. I moved closer—to the window because I thought this guy was crazy—masturbating in the library—and I didn't want to get up and leave, I thought he might follow me or something, so I just stayed there and tried to work. I tried to move away and tried to act nonchalant [laughs] but I was kind of nervous. I thought about getting up and leaving, but to do that I'd have to step right over him; I guess I wanted to melt into the wall like I wasn't even there, I didn't want him to notice me. I thought if he was crazy enough to do that, he would follow me. I didn't want to get up and go because I'd have to step over him and acknowledge that he was down there and I just wanted to hide and not even—like I wasn't even there. [You went back to your studying?] Well, I looked at it, I can remember trying to just keep on reading, and I really didn't—I *looked* at it, but it was like looking at just anything, not really concentrating.

If there is more than one person witnessing the exposure, the inattention may be more collaborative and even take the form of explicit advice.

> I was walking home from school and a group of my girlfriends, maybe six or so, and a station wagon pulled up next to the side of the curb where we were

and was driving alongside of us slowly. I looked over and saw he was exposed and thought, this is just what he wants so I won't look. I ignored him and walked on. My friends finally noticed and they stopped and stared in the window. I said, "you guys! Don't look at him, just ignore him." But they just stood there and I kept on walking.

A civil manner of inattention was used by one interviewee in an instance where she indicated being quite aware of her attempt to be circumspect.

At the bus stop . . . all I could do is sit there talking and trying to distract him from asking me questions again. I tried to sit very straight and also maintain a safe distance from him—about two feet—I tried not to look at him. I glanced over his side. I didn't bother to look exactly at what was in his hands but to me his hands were right . . . so I assume he was holding something I didn't—that would scare me. . . . As I said, I tried to be cold and distract him away from asking more questions and to give him the impression that I'm a very sensible girl and very cautious about him so I didn't look at him too much.

LEAVING

A final means of getting away to be noted here is when the interviewee withdrew her presence or got away by physically extricating herself from the immediate vicinity of the exposer. Rules of etiquette and decorum may be redefined in light of the fact that the exposure has the effect of disqualifying the exposer from the world of civility where more complex leave-taking rituals may be followed (Goffman, 1963: 110). Taking one's leave is guided by expediency and ecological factors rather than by the rules of polite interaction. Leaving may be aided or hampered by mechanical or architectural elements of public space. Leaving may require getting into or out of cars and buildings or perhaps slight bodily readjustments within a given space.

I was coming out of my apartment building . . . I noticed this man standing in the [vacant] lot. I went to my car and as soon as I got in I looked again, because I was aware of him. I was aware that he was there and I wanted to see what he was doing. And he came up to the window on the passenger side and exposed himself and . . . jerking off or whatever [term] you want to use for it—right there by my window on the passenger side. He didn't get in the car or anything like that. In fact I think I did reach back and lock my door and sit there and try to get my car started. I have a little foreign model and it takes ten minutes to warm up. Well, I was scared, but like, I just wanted to leave. But I was scared right then while he was doing it. It's kind of repulsive, plus I was scared he would try to get into my car. . . . [About how long was he at the side of your car?] As long as I took to get it started and leave.

Getting away may take the form of staying away if the exposure is anticipated, or if the actor has been encountered in the past and has thus acquired a disreputable biography.

> I used to go to school in LA and it took me an hour by streetcar and there was a black man who used to ride that particular streetcar. I used to see him almost everyday sitting in the back car. I used to walk past him and we used to stand in the back . . . we never really made an issue of it—"Oh, there he is again, Oh God. Let's get by him." We could get away by going to the back of the streetcar—a good ten feet. I would have never stood close to him. I would have removed myself somehow. I wouldn't have sat next to him. I would have stayed in the front car.

In this latter case the exposing alter had been encountered so routinely that he was regarded as an everyday life nuisance to be avoided in an almost mechanical fashion.

In withdrawing her presence the interviewee may have a specific or ad hoc destination that is associated with safety or escape. In the following case the interviewee changed her destination after she encountered the accosting actor a second time soon after the first.

> I was walking home just minding my own business, just concerned about getting home and I come up to this corner. I had to stop because there was a car going real slow. . . . He was way over on the right side and he turned left—I had to stop for him . . . and I looked in the window and the guy was there masturbating. I thought I'm going home and lock the door and it will be all gone. It won't be there any more . . . I just continued walking, "I'm just going to go home." When he came around the second time . . . I got paranoid. I thought I don't know if he knows that I live by myself. I can't go home. I went to a neighbor's house—she lives across the street. It doesn't bother me anymore, I mean I still have the feeling about it, but at the time it happened I was really upset, and when I did go home I called my mom. I stayed there [at her neighbor's] about twenty minutes, I stood there at the window to make sure he didn't come back. I mean I never thought about the possibility of him coming around the second time. I figured he came by and it happened and I would just go in my house and I would close my door and it would not be there anymore.

Getting away can also involve the continuation of a motion in progress but where those actions are continued more quickly. Several instances occurred while the interviewee was walking on a public path or street when accosted by the exhibitionist. In many instances the woman continued walking but defined it as faster in the direction away from the exposer, both in instances where they were not shaken up and where they described themselves as quite frightened.

> Well, I went to the [campus] library to see if it was open to get some books. And I parked the car . . . and there's a little dirt path that goes through the bushes that you have to go up to get to the top. And there was this guy there doing his thing, you know, in the bushes, so I kept going faster on down to the car. It scared me. [Did you do anything about it?] No, I ignored it. I had things to do yesterday so—it didn't shake me up that much.

> [From a nontaped interview]: Terri was on her way to the cafeteria to wait for her girlfriend to finish taking an examination she herself had just completed for their night college class. She heard noises and rustlings in the line of bushes along which she was walking but thought, "no, I'm paranoid, that's just in my mind." A man called her over and exposed himself and propositioned her. She screamed at him and walked away "very fast, I was afraid that if I ran I'd fall or something." The male walked along a path which paralleled the driveway she had turned onto still behind the row of bushes and still "murmuring things." She walked "completely out of my way to get back to class, walking where there were people and lights." She came across two "football jocks" and he stopped following her. "I was really scared."

The withdrawal of presence is most obvious when it takes the form of literally getting up and leaving, i.e., walking away when the person was not already walking away when first approached. In the instance mentioned earlier where the girl sat at the bus bench trying to distract the fellow from asking more questions, she finally said "oh no!" and left the bench.

> So I just ran away. [Nervous?] Nervous? No. I said Oh no! that is, I tried to tell him, even if you are trying to look for an object for sexual activity I said, "oh no" that's not me. And also, I said it to mean not me, *I* don't deserve something like that so I ran away. I turned back to see if he was following and if he was then I would have to turn back to Taco Bell, which is between this bus stop and the next bus stop I was running for. Fortunately, he wasn't there when I turned back. At the next bus stop it was dark, but I felt better then because I could see that there were no other people around.

Getting Help

Experiencing an exposure may entail seeking aid or an ally to help deal with the encounter. Such efforts to enlist aid when erotically accosted in public have gone largely unexamined. The decision to seek help can be seen as dependent upon the presumed availability of sympathetic others, and upon the sense that the main or side designs of the accosting alter are ambiguous and possibly malevolent. There is no clear line between the process of getting help and more simply telling others. Help may or may not be given without asking and may take the form of listening, calming the person, or calling the police. In the following case, for example, the interviewee sought the company of others nearby who themselves called the police.

> I was getting [ready] to go out. I [got] undressed and I was in the bathtub . . . and I was very busy, and there was a window at the back. There were other girls in the house, but there was no one else in this kind of suite [of the sorority house]. At one point I sort of glanced out and thought I saw some movement, and then I thought no, I didn't, you know, that's kind of silly. Anyway—I looked out and there was a guy out there—and he was masturbating. I kind of did a double take, I didn't even realize what was going on. At the time I thought "Oh my God, why did I even look at him?" I was not cool at all. I went screaming down the hall. I didn't even think, I had a telephone right there, I could have calmly gone out of the room and called and come back into the room and acted like nothing had happened. The others were very protective of me, they didn't ask what did he do, they were just protective.

Similarly, the company of especially capable others may be sought and it may in fact be they who take immediate and subsequent steps to do something about the incident.

> A really well-dressed guy, he had a good suit on . . . and about twenty-seven years old . . . and you know right away I sense something weird because he was just standing there in the dark . . . and I have to walk like that (around in front of him) by him, and as I turned the corner I noticed what he was doing . . . and it really freaked me out, because I didn't know if he was going to hurt me or what, so I ran past him, you know, and I ran right up the stairs to get my manager who is a policeman. And I got him and he comes tearing down with a gun and this guy jumps in a brand new El Dorado and takes off.

Reactions may take on the appearance of "seeking help" whereas other processes may be occurring. In the following case the interviewee as a teenager quickly told a nearby store manager not so much to enlist his aid but to "flirt" with him.

> The guy called us over to the car, he just said something like "Hey, come over here," or something. I went over. . . . He said something like "What do you think about this?" and we just cracked up! I don't know how that made him feel but we just cracked up. It was my idea to complain to the manager; he was a doll! He was embarrassed, and I thought that was neat, that I had embarrassed the man that I hoped to marry someday. But we thought it was funny, just funny. The police never came; the manager called the police. The guy stayed, he didn't take off, he was right in his car. We stayed in the store for half an hour and watched him; he stayed there and when we left he was still there. I couldn't control my laughter, I just stood there cracking up thinking, "What a fool!" That was my opinion.

The availability of others may vary with situational conditions such as the time of day, the nature and size of the involving enterprise (e.g., the number of people who normally work in any particular setting). In one case the interviewee called the police immediately with the accosting male still present because there "was nobody nearby."

> I was working in a doughnut shop in San Diego, in a secluded area, very dark, no lights, my first week (on the job), working graveyard, about two o'clock in the morning. A very good looking . . . man came up [nude but for a sports jacket]. . . . I was the only one there and it put me out a little, it pissed me off. There's nothing to do because you're there all by yourself, you can't run anywhere because there's no place to run and tell anybody. There's nobody there. He didn't have to worry about any clients coming in. He came up and asked me for a doughnut and I told him I was going to call the police and he left. . . . He just stood there until I turned my back, he just walked very casual. [Did you deliberate as to whether to call?] No, I was there by myself. I went straight to the phone. There was nobody nearby. I said I had an exhibitionist and wanted somebody to come by and check it out. They made a joke out of it, they thought it was very funny. [On the phone?] No, after they got there. I was surprised and [laughs] a little upset. Because I was all by myself, and I didn't know what this person—or what his intentions were. I know I was nervous the rest of the night. When I'd see my reflection in the window I'd jump.

Getting Involved

Whereas the above considerations center on efforts to remove themselves from the situation and to obtain help, there were several instances where those accosted aided in the focusing of the engagement by talking to or even approaching the exhibitionist. Thus to get closer or to get involved is to continue rather than to terminate the encounter and to converse with or otherwise aid in the focusing of mutual attention rather than to look away or leave. Obviously, interviewees may have aided in the focusing of the encounter and then opted to leave, get away, or get help. "Closeness" is here intended to refer not necessarily to physical proximity (although on rare occasion interviewees went over closer to watch *after* they knew of the exposure) but more to efforts on the part of the interviewee to address more directly the accoster and thereby interact more fully with him than in the previous instances cited. In this section we will examine those instances where the interviewee appears to have aided in (1) the focusing of the encounter by directly addressing the exposer or in some way "getting closer," and (2) the initiation of the processes of moral enterprise in which the activities of formal control agencies are invoked.

FOCUSING

In some instances interviewees would speak with or to the exposer and thus focus the encounter and socially make note of having "noticed." In the following case the interviewee was bothered by the incident yet claimed to have managed the trouble by calmly and cynically talking to him. She had first assumed she had chanced across his private auto-involvement but then was faced with a more elaborate production.

> I was outside [alone during a semester break on campus working in an art shop] and I was coming in the open doorway and there was a guy in the "graduate room" with the door open, and as soon as he saw me . . . he was just beating off with his pants unzipped . . . he saw me and turned around and went the other way and I figured, "Oh, caught him!" and he didn't really want me seeing him and I thought he was hiding from somebody [having ducked into the graduate room] and [he] felt really ashamed. He probably was thinking this is my chance and I got to let it out.
>
> And I went back to my stuff [art project] and I looked up and there he was with *all* his clothes off in the doorway; he was doing the same bit and I applauded and I said, "OK, very nice, that was very good, and now you can put it away." He was hiding his head behind the wall of the doorway. And I got up and said, "I think I'll call the campus police if you won't leave 'cause this isn't a show I want to watch." And I kept walking this way towards the door and he kept hiding his head. I had already *seen* his face! I just said I'll call campus police, that's all there is to it—I just didn't want him there. . . . And I just began to feel really strange. . . . After that I didn't come here unless somebody else was with me, I'd recruit somebody to come with me.

As noted earlier, "conversation" with the accosting male is usually minimal or nonexistent. Where it does occur it is in almost every instance to control or condemn the untoward act. In the earlier instance where two women were riding on the bike trail and were exposed to by a youth the interviewee's girlfriend had said to the youth, "You're weird! You're just really weird!" Similarly, in the recollections of one interviewee, a mother directly "confronted" the man who had exposed himself to her and possibly the children.

> It happened at the library with my mother and my younger sister. It was a really hot day. My mother said, "you kids wait here and I'll go get the car" . . . [she] walked out and [saw] this man was in the bushes. She got really annoyed and went over and said, "well, now I have your license plate number and I'm going to the police." She had a confrontation with him. She had a confrontation with [another man] where she said she was going to report him and he said, "Oh no, please, my wife would be really upset, she doesn't know about this!"

This form of actually approaching the exposing alter is most dramatically illustrated in the following instance where the interviewee chased the man down an alley.

> Barbara was leaving work in the afternoon when a man who had been "waiting" on the other side of the parking lot unzipped his pants and exposed himself after walking a short ways toward her. She was getting into her car when this happened and she became "furious" at the fellow's actions. She said that she rarely "blows up" but when she does she can "get violent." She said that this was one of those times and she literally drove down the alley in pursuit of the man who had exposed himself. She said that she fully intended to "run him over!" She drove for a block down the alley before she lost sight of him. She thought she might have recognized him from around the neighborhood. She went home and told her mother who told her that she should call the police because of the harm that might come to the little children in the neighborhood.

Laughter is one way in which the encounter is rendered seemingly harmless by refusing to appear to take it seriously.

> I was in the parking lot at [State College] coming out of the library. I see this really odd looking man standing beside his car. He looks just like Yul Brynner; shaved head, sun glasses, a really funny shirt on. I thought "Oh oh, he's really funny looking." All of a sudden he comes out from the car and flashes. It just struck me funny and I burst out laughing. I thought it was really comical.

Similarly, the event may strike the person as "funny" but still seem to require some remedial action. In public places the untoward encounter may be at once amusing and out of place. Spatial arrangements may afford the aforementioned sense of protection and thus evoke an amused reaction.

> My cousin and I were at a restaurant and we sat right next to the windows . . . and a guy pulled alongside and I looked again and I thought, "Wow! What a trip!" and she looked and she was really embarrassed, and I said "I'm going to go out there!" So I went out there to get his license plate number and he drove off. She was really embarrassed and hid her face. . . . Ordinarily I wouldn't have gone out there, maybe it's because I felt kind of protective of her. She was still laughing and she said, "No, no, don't!" [Why do you think he left?] I guess he didn't want me to get his license plate number. I doubt if he thought I was going out there to talk to him. I remember thinking I wouldn't go outside the door, because maybe he's got a gun or something. I got to the door and stopped because he drove off. I thought it was funny, we thought it was funny, it's not really a threat, you know? . . . I felt protected there in the restaurant.

Thus it appears that the accosted person may choose to pursue or focus the encounter in order to chastise or challenge the "symbolic assailant" (Skolnick, 1966: 45). In an encounter where it would normally be assumed that those exposed to would "keep their distance" and leave if at all possible, women may focus the encounter and, in a sense, get closer through talk and movement. But as has been seen, getting involved can refer to a more extended means of handling the situation when, for example, outside groups or agencies become involved in the encounter. Not wanting to get involved is a frequently cited reason for not reporting one's own victimization and it is that curious twist on the notion of involvement that we will now consider.

REPORTAGE AND MORAL ENTERPRISE

In addition to getting help the process of telling others may by design or effect result in the involvement of the police.[9] In ten of the more than forty instances to which we had access the police were in fact called. The interviewee may or may not have desired the involvement of the police when others were told. If the police were to become involved at all it was usually in the first few minutes following the exposure or following the notification of others who may have taken it upon themselves to call the police or to convince the interviewee that she should call them. The concept of moral enterprise (Emerson and Messinger, 1972) in the present case can be seen as the steps taken which culminate in the act of notifying or acquiescing in the notification of the police or other official control agents. Our impression is that our interviewees did not so much "complain" to the police and others as simply tell them or seek their company. The cases in which the police were called regarding indecent exposure as described by our interviewees suggest that the decision to call and the calling itself are often tentative and collaborative efforts. The notification of the authorities is not so much a response to a sense of moral outrage or an attempt to recoup "losses" as it is often a process in which the woman who was accosted is chided or told by others that the police should be called. For example, the art student who applauded the "show" of a nude male ran into someone who worked in the building as she ran out of the room.

> The lab tech came in and I told him about it and he told me I should call the campus police. And [he] called the campus police and I told them about it and they came and lugged me around the campus looking for him. [At first

were you going to call the police?] No, I saw no need to. I wasn't going to. He said it should be done. [Why?] He just said he might bug somebody else.

In another instance the interviewee and her brother had been exposed to while waiting in an automobile for their father. When told of the incident by the interviewee, the father drove her around the area looking for the man. He was found driving a car at a nearby shopping center and followed onto a freeway where the license plate number was taken and the girl positively identified the man. The father then drove to the police station where he reported the incident, giving the police the exposer's license plate number. It was clearly the father's persistence that led to the reportage.

SUMMARY

Interviews with women who had encountered an exhibitionist were conducted to examine the retrospective social meanings associated with the experience and the strategies employed in dealing with or managing what in most instances was thought to be an untoward event. Most interviewees felt in retrospect that they had not been hurt by the exposer and by this they commonly meant that they had not been touched or violently assaulted. The exposure tends to be viewed as an esoteric and adverse auto-involvement (Goffman, 1963) where the clues to the exhibitionist's commitment to an auto focus are ambiguous. Interviewees tend to indicate that the event did not so much harm them as surprise them.[10] The event is thought not to have been dangerous but rather weird and even inconvenient.

> It is not that kind of thing that is going to harm you that much. An assault like that is not nearly as harmful as other verbal and mental and emotional assaults that we experience every day.

> It's inconvenient but a lot of things are inconvenient. I guess I'm not so concerned with somebody that's going to do some sort of exhibitionist thing as I am with somebody that's going to carry through.

> Well, as long as he doesn't hurt me or harm me, I guess they can do pretty much what they want. . . . It's not bad at all. It's kind of humorous, strange. [Harmful or harmless?] Yeah, I did think he was harmless because I didn't think there was anything that was going to happen to me.

We discovered no single context of the occurrence short of almost always having occurred in a public place. The most common context of the encounters to which we had access involved public streets and automobiles, but encounters also took place in commercial establishments, front yards, sorority houses and dormitories, and on college campuses. Although each of our interviewees in a technical sense had encountered an exhibitionist, we discovered no single definition of the incident. Over-arching labels such as prank, assault, inconvenience, and outlets were used to describe both the same and different experiences.

We found no single affective response to the events. In some ways the public priapic overtures were quite similar and yet interviewees varyingly reacted with repulsion, fear, nervousness, amusement, sang-froid, humor, and anger. There was no single way of dealing with the encounter. Management strategies ranged from leaving immediately or calling the police to doing nothing by ignoring or seeming to ignore the incident. In general the social meanings associated with this type of erotic offensive-ness and sexual victimization centered on the perceived accidental nature of the interviewee's involvement. The ambiguity of the events was managed through getting away, getting help, and getting involved.

In light of the above points—which emphasize the importance of the social context of the untoward erotic act in producing the meanings associated with it—we can suggest the following generalizations. First, given the collaboration sometimes involved in the decision to call the police, we are even further convinced that the naturally occurring and if possible the in situ experiences of sexual offenses require considerably more attention if we are to understand offensiveness. The turn of events which results in the formal notification of police is little understood; and to rely simply upon sexual crimes known to the police for analysis is to neglect the critical processes and the social context which result in the decision to notify. Similarly, the examination of only those cases known to the police (or clinics and institutions) will likely distort the degree and nature of the offensiveness or indecency concerning public encounters. It appears that the very understandings which define the appropriateness and inappropriateness of social approaches and overtures in public places aids in the concealment and low visibility of an event that may prove surprisingly common. While the incidence of the phenomenon is not at issue here, we can expect that untoward alters who violate the rules of public order by acting weird or strange are themselves accounted for by the apparent victim and thus explained, cognitively managed, and—as in most cases examined here—dispensed with as essentially harmless. The definitions of public places as diffuse settings frequented by a host of untoward types aid in defining the untoward and the unexpected as something that just happens when it is experienced.

Second, there exists the need to study comparatively both erotic and nonerotic accosting behaviors in different types of settings. While this study has examined erotic victimization unrestricted by setting, the importance of the specific conditions and meanings associated with specific settings (of work, leisure, and privacy) is such that public accostings might be better understood through field studies of actors and activities per setting.

NOTES

1. Medical views and definitions of exhibitionism vary. Arieff and Rotman (1942: 525, 527) define it as "the willful exhibiting of one's genital organs usually in public places . . . (and) the opposite sex must look and be shocked. The patient may masturbate or ejaculate if the shock to the observer is great, thus completing an otherwise inadequate sexual act." The psychodynamic literature draws an important distinction between exhibitionism per se and sexual exhibitionism. Exhibitionistic behaviors may include a wide range of behaviors which are thought to be intended to draw attention to the self, such as stammering and "tantrums" (Christoffel, 1936). Mohr et al. (1964: 116) define exhibitionism as "the expressed impulse to expose the male genital organ to an unsuspecting female as a final sexual gratification. . . . The exhibitionist derives his gratification from the reaction of the object (victim) to the sight offered, but does not attempt any further contact" (also see East, 1924).

2. The press, on the other hand, tends to describe the offense largely in terms of legalistic or criminal classifications, tending to neglect altogether the perceptions and reactions of the victim. For example,

> "A 26 year old woman reported to police Saturday that a male exposed himself to her in the art library at 2:40 p.m. She called police ten minutes later and reported the incident. An officer responded immediately and was given a description of the suspect. A search of the immediate area was fruitless, but as the officer expanded the search to (a parking structure) he observed a male who fit the woman's description. The officer requested the man to come with him. He complied and was taken back to the woman. She identified the suspect and placed him under citizen's arrest at 3:30 p.m. on charges of indecent exposure. The officer transported the suspect to West City jail where he was booked. Bail was set at $500" (*Daily Bruin,* Friday, April 28, 1972, p. 2).

3. We have decided to retain the use of the term "reactions" for the sense-making operations of our interviewees as they recall their own thoughts and efforts to deal with the encounter. A problem arises, however, when the use of the term assumes that there is a standardized stimulus to which women were reacting. The very point is that there was no such standardized stimulus but rather the experience of an encounter usually defined as ambiguous and untoward, which in some fashion must be handled or managed. Our uses of the concepts of erotic

offensiveness and sexual victimization are but introductory and heuristic devices by which to introduce an alternative to assuming that the erotically offensive stimulus necessarily offends or necessarily generates a "victim."

4. We use the term exposure rather than exhibitionism because the term exhibitionism carries with it several clinical assumptions regarding the interests and motives of the man exposing himself—an area of inquiry outside the scope of this paper.

5. There is precedent for a nonlegalistic use of the term victim (see, for example, Gagnon, 1965) and our use of the term here refers obviously not to the judicial classification of offenders and victims, but to the ostensibility of its appropriateness in a situation which could be and at times was conceived of as illegal.

6. The limitations of this approach are clear. Most importantly, we cannot estimate the effect of intervening time upon the accounts of the incident. We have taken the accounts of reactions at face value for the sake of the analysis (see Schurtz, 1960).

7. Arieff and Rotman (1942) examined 100 cases of clinical exhibitionism; all were males. The female cases involving exhibitionistic behaviors were diagnosed as transvestism and alcoholism. The exhibitionists in their study tended to be white and single, 33 of them picked public places, "such as the beach, zoo, theater, street car, school, park or in an auto on the street or alley" (1942: 524). The remaining cases occurred in or near the home of the exhibitionist.

8. It is difficult to describe the affective reactions of victims, especially when using retrospective accounts of a very fleeting encounter, and when the meanings of the incident in part require a reation-seeking accoster. Our tendency was to rely upon the more freely given adjectives of our interviewees rather than to pursue more directly the issue of whether they were shocked or not shocked.

9. Working police procedures regarding this type of offense and legal reasoning regarding the "normal" aspects of the case have yet to be examined in depth. When a campus police department was approached regarding the research we were told that the women students reporting the offense would probably be too embarrassed to talk about it: "Some girls, however, you can't stop them from telling all the details, they just keep talking, like they enjoy it. It seems like they get their kicks from telling about it. You get both kinds."

Another officer, a female sergeant, said that women are often afraid to press charges and the officers may therefore try "to remind her that exposing is only the start," and that as the "guy gets less and less of a thrill from exposing himself" he will then become physical and perhaps rape someone.

10. Some interviewees suggested that the only real danger or harm would come if the man approached a child: "I don't know if you can consider the person really sick or ... the only thing I think is maybe dangerous is if he shows it to a little kid ... a little girl who sees this, who's never seen."

REFERENCES

ARIEFF, A. and D. ROTMAN (1942) "One hundred cases of indecent exposure." J. of Nervous and Mental Diseases 96: 523-529.

CHRISTOFFEL, H. (1936) "Exhibitionism and exhibitionists." International J. of Psychoanalysis 17: 321-345.

EAST, W. N. (1924) "Observations on exhibitionism." Lancet 23: 370-375.

EMERSON, R. M. and S. MESSINGER (1972) "A sociology of trouble." Presented to the annual meetings of the Society for the Study of Social Problems, New Orleans, Louisiana.

GAGNON, J. (1965) "Female child victims of sex offenses." Social Problems 13: 176-192.

GOFFMAN, E. (1963) Behavior in Public Places. New York: Free Press.

KANIN, E. J. (1969) "Selected dyadic aspects of male sex aggression." J. of Sex Research 5 (February): 12-28.

KIRKPATRICK, C. and E. KANIN (1957) "Male sex aggression on campus." Amer. Soc. Rev. 22: 52-58.

LOFLAND, L. H. (1973) A World of Strangers: Order and Action in Urban Public Space. New York: Basic Books.

MOHR, J. W., R. E. TURNER, and M. B. JERRY (1964) Pedophilia and Exhibitionism: A Handbook. Toronto, Can.: Univ. of Toronto Press.

SCHURTZ, W. G. (1960) "Interviewing the sex offender's victims." J. of Criminal Law and Criminology 50: 448-452.

SKOLNICK, J. H. (1966) Justice Without Trial. New York: John Wiley.

TAYLOR, F. H. (1947) "Observations on some cases of exhibitionism." J. of Mental Sci. 93: 631-638.

ZURCHER, L. A., Jr., R. G. KIRKPATRICK, R. CUSHING, and C. BOWMAN (1971) "The anti-pornography campaign: a symbolic crusade." Social Problems 19 (Fall): 217-238.